Betty Fairchild & Nancy Hayward

Now That You Know

What Every Parent Should Know About Homosexuality

A Harvest/HBJ Book
Harcourt Brace Jovanovich, Publishers
San Diego   New York   London

Requests for permission to make copies
of any part of the work should be mailed to:
Permissions, Harcourt Brace Jovanovich,
Publishers, Orlando, FL 32887.

The authors would like to thank the following
for permission to quote from their work:

Sheed & Ward, Inc. for
The Church and the Homosexual,
Copyright, 1976 by John J. McNeill, S.J. / Distributed by
Sheed Andrews and McMeel.

The Rt. Reverend Paul Moore, Jr. for the statement he issued
in 1977 to Episcopal vestries in New York City.

The Paulist Press for *Human Sexuality: New Directions in American
Catholic Thought* by Anthony Kosnik, William Carroll, Agnes Cunningham, Ronald Modras, and James Schulte, © 1977 by The Catholic Theological Society of America. Reprinted by permission of The Paulist Press.

Library of Congress Cataloging in Publication Data

Fairchild, Betty.
Now that you know.

Bibliography: p.
1. Homosexuals—United States—Family relationships.
I. Hayward, Nancy, joint author. II. Title.
HQ76.3.U5F33   301.41'57   78-22251
ISBN 0-15-667702-4

Printed in the United States of America

F G H I J

*To all our gay children—
yesterday, today, and tomorrow.*

Acknowledgments

The stories and letters included in this book are about real people, and their stories are in their own words. In most cases, when first names only are used, they and the identifying details have been changed to maintain personal privacy. However, when both first and last names are given, they are the real names of those individuals, used with their permission.

Our heartfelt thanks and appreciation go to all the women and men who sent us their stories, many of which we regret we were unable to include. However, every personal account has enhanced our perceptions and understanding and, in so doing, has been a valuable contribution to the book. In addition, we are most grateful to the innumerable friends and associates whose sustaining interest and support have helped in various ways in the production of this book.

—Betty Fairchild and Nancy Hayward

Contents

Now That You Know

1

Now That You Know

It happened on a snowy Sunday morning in early 1970. Glenn, seventeen, and I were home alone (Ellen, older, was married and living away; Nicki, younger, was visiting a friend overnight). I was outside shoveling out the car, while Glenn slept. Then, to my surprise, he called out the door. "You coming in soon?"

"*Up* already?" I said with some irony. "I'll be in soon. Or—you come do this for me, huh?" He disappeared. I shoveled.

A few minutes passed; he stuck his head out again. "Are you coming in, Mom? I gotta talk to you."

A small alarm went up—I abandoned my task and went inside, taking off my boots and jacket and putting on a cheerful face. Glenn was not in sight.

"What's up?" I called. "Had breakfast yet?"

He tore through the hall, his face oddly red, mumbling, "Yes. No—I'm not hungry."

We settled in the living room with coffee. I had no glimmer of what was on his mind, but he certainly had my attention.

"I don't know how to tell you—" he began, his voice breaking. "It's too awful." After a moment, thinking of "the worst," I said, "Is Laura pregnant?"

Glenn rubbed at his eyes. "No—it's worse than that."

My mind went blank, casting about for terrible things. "Are you in trouble with the police?"

"No . . . Mom—" he stopped and blew his nose. "Mom, it's—well, it's . . . I'm homosexual."

Everything in me shrieked NO! and my mind raced idiotically. You can't be! . . . if only Laura *were* pregnant . . . no grandchildren . . . awful! . . . can't be . . . what did I do wrong . . . NO!

"Well," I said, at last, "it's not the end of the world, honey."

But inside me, it was.

Glenn told me he was gay when he was a senior in high school. He was a wonderful young man, interested especially in music and drama. He was not dating—although Laura was a close friend—and like most mothers, I'd been hoping he would soon. But I never had an inkling that he might be gay; in those days I didn't even think in those terms. I'd never even known anyone who was gay.

Glenn and I talked for hours that Sunday as morning passed into afternoon. He said he'd known this since junior high, and even before, but had never had a gay friend until recently when he and Ted, a friend at school, had discovered each other.

As we talked then and in later weeks, I felt like a sponge, soaking up everything Glenn had to say, anxious to know, and squeezing a few drops of comfort out of the vain hope that I might hear him say at last that it was "only a phase," that he was "OK now."

For weeks, perhaps months, I carried this Terrible Secret with the weight of sickness within me. All the dreadful things I'd heard, vague as they were, churned in my mind; my son was one of "those people." On the surface, life went on as usual, but I believed and felt that nothing would ever be the same.

Like most nongay people, I equated homosexuality with SEX, and I tortured myself with unpleasant thoughts when Glenn was out in the evenings. (I hadn't had the same worries when my daughters dated—although I might well have!)

So six months later, when Glenn left for college in the Southwest, I was relieved not to have to know where he was when, as it were, and could deal a little more rationally with the subject of homosexuality. But still, I had a lot of concerns and fears, and a lot of learning to do.

This is the beginning of Betty's story, but it could happen to any of us. We may read it in a carefully worded letter, the tone anguished or defiant, or both. It may happen over the telephone: "I tried to tell you when I was home, but I just couldn't face it." Sometimes it has to be a hasty revelation in the car when your daughter picks you up from work, so that she can break the news before you see her this evening on television speaking at the Gay Pride rally. But however it happens, it comes down to our hearing essentially this: "Mom, Dad, I have something to tell you. I'm gay. . . ."

Perhaps, like the two of us, you know what it means to learn that your child is homosexual. However our child tells us, whatever the words that finally convey the message, they are rarely spoken lightly and even more rarely heard easily. When our children "come out" to us, it is often their final exit from the closet. Friends, associates, possibly brothers and sisters may already know, but it usually seems hardest to tell Mom and Dad.

It can happen to any of us, and it has happened to thousands of families who never expected it, who never even considered the possibility. Some women and men can accept innate differences in people, including their own children. We know several parents who responded to the big announcement with: "We knew it all the time. We wanted you to tell us when you were ready." But most of us feel shock, disbelief, even horror. We catch ourselves hoping we'll wake up and find that it was a bad dream. We fight off recurring images of bizarre sex scenes featuring our own beautiful children in degrading, perhaps dangerous, circumstances. We want help, support, sympathy from loved ones and trusted friends, someone to help us bear the pain—and yet we shudder at the thought of telling anyone.

Suddenly the son or daughter we thought we knew is a stranger with a secret life. Suppose anyone from the office, the church, the club found out about this terrible thing! How could we face their polite masks, knowing that gossip spreads, dreading to think how fast and how far it may travel. It's hard to face the future knowing that the wedding everyone anticipated will never take place, that the babies will never come home to be petted and praised and shown off to relatives. Their cousins will get married, as well as their friends from school. How will we be able to pretend we don't care?

Often the guilt is the worst part. Where did we go wrong? How much of this did we bring on ourselves? Some parents try to reject that burden by transferring it to the child. These are the ones who react with: "How could you do a thing like this to us!" Or even: "You did this to spite us!" And in all too many cases: "We don't want anything more to do with you. As far as we're concerned, we'd rather you were dead!" Some parents react with incredible viciousness —one woman drove her son out of the house when he came home to try to talk with her. Later his older brothers came around to beat him up, warning him to stay away from Mom from then on.

Some parents cast around for outside influences. "That friend of yours that hangs around here taught you to be this way!" One father sadly said to his daughter: "Was it that boy you went with when you were sixteen?" And some throw up the defenses right away: "I never raised you like this! I took you to church, taught you what's right!" We hear some stories that would be funny if they didn't show such tragic ignorance. One mother went to the silverware drawer right away and began to take out one spoon, one fork, and so forth, saying that her daughter wouldn't be able to handle the dishes or eat with the rest of the family.

Others try to adjust to the guilt by looking around in the past for areas where they might have failed. If my husband had spent more time with the kids! If I had watched my son more carefully for signs—made him get more involved in sports. If only I had insisted that my daughter wear more feminine clothes! Some wonder what odious failure could have brought such a terrible punishment from the Almighty. One very religious mother berated herself at length in a letter to her son; she said she had usurped her husband's proper place as head of the household and this was her retribution for defying God's plan.

The chances are that most of us have reacted with some of these thoughts and questions, perhaps verbalized, perhaps not. It isn't easy, given our backgrounds and the endless subliminal messages thrown at us, to hear that our child is different. The revelation assaults everything we thought we knew about our child, and about the way things *are,* and certainly the way they *ought* to be.

Yet none of those reactions is very useful or constructive —either for us as parents or for our children. There are better things to consider: What, if anything, can I do to help my child? What is the best way to respond to my son? What do I need to know, and where can I get accurate information? Whom can I talk to? What does "being lesbian" mean to my daughter? And most important of all, what does my child need most from me, right now?

There really aren't any sensible answers to the hysterical

outbursts, but there are positive and helpful answers to the latter questions. There are things you can do for your child; there are loving ways to respond (even if you don't yet "understand"); there is much to be learned about how gay men and women fit into our society, what their needs and hopes are, what being gay means to your particular child— and what she or he needs from you at the moment of revelation and thereafter.

In the past it has not been an easy process, responding in a constructive way to this assault on our deeply ingrained beliefs and attitudes, because we have not had much help or information. But there's no need for us to continue to remain in unnecessary distress. With love and forthrightness, all of us can go through this process constructively, as so many parents already have, as we have.

Again, Betty's story:

About a year after Glenn went away to school, the change occurred—not in my son, but in me. By this time Glenn was living in Berkeley, and I went out there to visit him and to see some of California for the first time. It was a brand-new experience for me.

During my ten days there I became intensely aware of how little I knew of the many ways people act, think, and live. I met a number of Glenn's friends—people quite different from any I had known. They were interesting, active, and capable men and women, some of them most endearing. And I found that my assumptions about how people ought to live were really put on the line, assumptions not only about the area of sexual orientation, but about political and social views and a wide variety of personal lifestyles. It was an exciting, and a shattering, experience for me, one that allowed me to put the pieces together again as a more compassionate, educated, and understanding person.

Not surprisingly, perhaps, one of the most significant ways in which Berkeley changed my life was that very soon after my return, I realized that I was totally comfortable with homosexuality, with Glenn, and with other gay people I was getting to know and care about.

As for my other children, I found that Glenn had already told his older sister, Ellen, during one of her visits home, before he told me. She had been very supportive (although at that time she did not know much about homosexuality) and had helped him find a psychologist to talk to—not to change but to sort out his feelings and to validate himself as a good person.

Glenn and his one-year-younger sister had always been very close, and perhaps because of this he did not want Nicki to know at the time he told me. But a few months after he'd left for college, he wrote that it would be all right to tell her. I set the scene carefully for this crucial announcement.

I said, "I have something to tell you about Glenn."

"What? Is he homosexual?" Nicki said, adding, "I kind of thought so."

Since then, Glenn and Nicki (and later Ellen) have had many mutual friends, and most of them seem to have no problem with anyone's sexual orientation.

Nancy's story:

I come from a somewhat different background than Betty; I was brought up in New York City where the residents pride themselves on accepting even the most bizarre differences in people. I became more clearly aware of homosexuality in the late forties, when I visited the summer resort on Fire Island. There, as a child, I was fascinated by the large enclave of well-to-do gay men who were well liked and highly respected by the other summer people. My interest in homosexuality continued to the point that I later wrote a college paper on the subject.

I was fairly well prepared, then, to accept my daughter's revelation. Avril told me she was gay at the end of her freshman year in college; I asked her at once whether it might not be "just a stage." She looked at me pityingly, regretting such deplorable ignorance in an educated woman, and said, "No, Ma. That's not how it is. You're thinking about old-fashioned Freudian theories. Nobody believes that anymore. Let me give you some books." When she went west for the summer to stay with her new lover, she left me with *Lesbian/Woman* by Del Martin and Phyllis Lyon, and Germaine Greer's *The Female Eunuch,* as well as some periodical articles.

Avril told me that she had "really tried to get into men" during her college freshman year. She had indeed written us about an engaging, somewhat older man for whom she had a lot of respect and whom she was seeing a lot. I had wondered at the time what he might be like; I could never really imagine what kind of man Avril would be comfortable with. Later I found out that this is typical—most gay men and women have some experience with the opposite sex before deciding that gay relationships suit them better.

The reading and the good communication that has always existed in our family made adjustment fairly easy for us. Abby, then eight years old, was disappointed about not getting little nieces and nephews to pamper, because she had been hoping that her sister would be getting married soon. She managed to comfort herself by vowing to raise a large brood of her own as soon as possible. I simply explained to her that Avril loved other women rather than men, and she accepted it as she would any other inexplicable foible of this family she loves. As time went on she picked up more information from the talk at home, though she seldom asked direct questions.

Looking back now, in retrospect I can see that it really wasn't too much of a shock for any of us. We had always sensed that Avril never seemed to fit easily into the girl games and activities that interested her classmates. As a child she hadn't made friends readily—there was a kind of aloofness about her that put other children off. In high school she had her music. She and her brother Matt, who is almost two years younger, had moved in a young musicians' circle—the endless round of rehearsals, lessons, practicing, concerts, auditions had kept her busy and at least superficially content. I remember her saying to me once, "When I have my cello with me I know who I am; I'm a musician." Matt's best friend at that time had been a young gay pianist whom we all respected, and both of them had known gays at music camp, so there was no shock associated with the idea of homosexuality per se. We all realized that Avril would be going through a lot of changes as she realigned her life, so we adopted a more or less wait-and-see attitude.

After her announcement to the family Avril began to open up like a flower. She gave up music, feeling that it drew her too much inward and away from more valuable human contacts. She made friends, dozens of them, and learned to meet people on her own terms instead of those society had compelled in the past. She stood up straighter and resumed the active sports she had loved as a child. She had her lank, stringy hair cut so that it curled all over her head in naturally golden waves. She began to take an interest in clothes, learning how to develop a style that suited her trim, boyish build and new self-image. And she went back to school in a field that thrilled her—classical literature.

Betty mentioned at the beginning of this chapter that she had hoped Glenn might outgrow his interest in men, and of course I thought the same at first. But actually it was my husband and I who soon outgrew the idea that our child might move on toward a heterosexual orientation. The idea ceased to seem very relevant after a while. Whatever she was doing in bed, or with whom, it was surely more her own business than ours. When Avril told us recently that there was a man in her life, her father and I said, "Oh? And what does he do?" It seemed important that she had a new and significant friend, but not particularly important what sex he or she happened to be.

Quite a few parents, usually those who don't communicate freely with their gay children, never reach that point. They go on hoping against hope that the "right guy" or the "right girl" will show up and make the miracle happen. Or they seize upon the idea that some sort of psychotherapy or counseling will bring a "cure," even though there is seldom anything to be gained by that approach. In our experience and that of our friends, trying to change usually does more harm than good.

The major problem is usually one of understanding that everyone is unique and has to follow his or her own best judgment—which is why we felt so strongly about writing this book. So many parents think of the terrible myths and stereotypes they've heard about "queers"—lonely, alienated people who frequent seedy bars and tenderloin districts looking for a pickup. All those pitiful lost souls our mothers told us about, lurking in rest rooms, luring youngsters into performing degenerate acts; does this mean that our child will turn out to be one of "them"? Our daughter in men's clothes, our son limp-wristed, ending up unloved, unwanted, a human derelict?

Well, of course it doesn't, unless that child happens to be seriously neurotic and gives up on living—a state hardly unique to homosexuals.

Neither Betty nor I could ever see Avril or Glenn as one of "them." But it wasn't until we began working with gay people and learning to love them that we found out why. It's because "they" don't exist. Our children aren't like "them"—on the contrary, "they" are exactly like our children: shy or bold, uninhibited or repressed, boisterous or quiet, generous or stingy, dependent or supportive, just like everybody. And, of course, that's what this book is all about.

As time went on, both of us drifted gradually toward activism. As Betty has pointed out, the first people we met were our children's friends. Avril has always brought home the new women in her life—she is proud of them and proud of her family, and she wants all of us to appreciate each other. The more I saw of these remarkable young women, the faster the stereotypes dropped away. I found out that lesbians don't want to be men, that as a group they aren't at all shy and withdrawn or aggressively masculine and "butch." On the contrary, many are poised and lovely enough to be homecoming queens. They would come home with Avril for dinner or a weekend and listen to the household banter, the family jokes we toss around, the easy fun we have together, and say, "Wow, I wish I could be open with my family and friends like this!"

I visited their houses because my daughter and her friends lived in them. I patronized their jewelry and craft businesses and the art galleries because Avril thought so highly of their work that I went to look, and sometimes stayed to buy. I bought feminist literature from a women's book distributor for classes I was teaching at a girls' vocational school, and picked up public-health materials for my students at the same time. I bought books that Avril had recommended at the bookstores. My husband, Tod, and I went with her friends to concerts of women's music and took our ten-year-old daughter with us because other women were bringing their kids. Nothing happens at a concert by and for women that shouldn't happen in your living room, at least not on a Friday night in Washington, D.C. The music is lively and the audience high-spirited—a good evening of family fun.

And the bars. There's a scene you might think a mother would want to stay away from. Not a bit of it. Let me tell you about the time I took my mother-in-law to a lesbian club in southeast Washington.

Tod's mother is a native of Oklahoma. She visited us one summer, a year or so after Avril came out, and we took that occasion to explain her granddaughter's sexual orientation. Now Mother is nobody's fool. She had figured out the situation for herself already, but there were a lot of myths to explode and it took a certain amount of exposure to Avril's life-style to bring her thinking up to date. Late in the summer I decided she was ready for the whole dose. I invited her to go into Washington with me on a Thursday evening, when I knew live entertainment would be featured at Avril's favorite club.

I had been to the Club Madame a few times before. It's a little more commercial there these days, with slick floor shows on weekends, but back in 1974 the atmosphere at Madame's reminded me of nothing so much as my dorm at Bryn Mawr. There were long tables with folding chairs and smaller round tables with checkered cloths. The room was comfortably lit, with a smallish dance floor, a jukebox, and a bar along one side where a couple of policemen usually lounged among the customers. No doubt they were supposed to be patrolling the place, but I suspect they hung around because they enjoyed the atmosphere. A few other men were circulating quietly near the back of the room and at the bar. Some of them danced together to the jukebox, along with the lesbian couples and an occasional straight visitor. In general it's impossible to tell who is who, except for the young lovers who hold hands and cuddle. The older women tend to be more restrained—there's a lot of kissing as friends come and go, but little overt sexuality. Groups mix, talk, exchange introductions, and look over the newcomers as they enter. Most of the younger crowd wear jeans.

The night we went one of Avril's closest friends was leaving just as we got there. She had already met my mother-in-law, so she kissed us both and presented me with a can of maple syrup she had brought as a present from Vermont. As we sat down at a small table another old friend came over to hug me and be introduced to Tod's mother. Avril was sitting across the room with friends and didn't notice us come in.

When the motherly looking waitress came over to take our order I asked her to take drinks to Avril and Barbara, mentioning that the blond one was my daughter. The waitress remarked, "My, you don't look old enough to have a grown daughter!" Mother popped up: "And I'm the grandmother!" More admiring noises and exclamations about her youthful appearance. I couldn't have been more tickled at how well the evening was going. The two older women beamed at each other.

The jukebox stopped playing, the lights went down, and a singer was announced. A young woman in jeans and a plaid shirt performed songs she had written herself in a country-western manner. Her style was witty and fast-paced, with effective guitar accompaniment. The audience was attentive and applause followed each number. Announcements of events in the lesbian community followed the set, and we left; Avril came over to hug us good-bye.

Personally I think that visiting the right, carefully chosen bar is a fine way to introduce relatives to gay life, but of course it might not be everybody's cup of tea. My own mother, a politically liberal New Yorker, had no trouble with the idea of a lesbian granddaughter. She recently told me about how, at a meeting of her Episcopal vestry, she defended her bishop's ordination of a gay woman priest. One of the other vestrymen had been shocked at the bishop's action and said so, but my mother spoke up for him and afterward the group voted almost unanimously in favor of her position. Needless to say, she was pleased as punch, especially since she happened to be the only woman serving on the vestry at that time.

My father took the news pretty easily, though he surprised me by asking whether Avril was "the man" or "the woman." He was referring to a traditional idea about lesbians which assumes a pattern of aggression and passivity in all sexual relationships. This phenomenon is disappearing today, though it does still exist, especially among women of lower socioeconomic background. I explained to my father that role-playing is in bad repute these days. Lesbian-feminist couples try to avoid stereotypical behavior by setting up the idea of an equal partnership as the ideal. They make important decisions together and take turns in lovemaking; if one is temperamentally more aggressive she may purposely encourage the other to play a more dominant role, and vice versa. Even after explaining all of this I'm not sure whether my father understood how that could work, but anyhow, I tried.

When you've grown up believing a myth, as my father did, it can be hard to shake. Since I was raised in a city where most behavior is accepted without judgment, I had never been exposed to many of the most common myths about gays. By now, since I've been doing research and working for gay rights, I think I must have heard them all. Especially the one about the destruction of the American family—as if homosexuality were so unbelievably tempting that young people have only to meet an admired gay man or woman to be irrevocably drawn into a gay life-style. Of course the corollary to that is that gays are interested in converting children, although no one who has ever been intimate with gay people could believe that for a second. Officers in the Mattachine Society, one of the oldest homophile organizations in the United States, have expressed their opinion of the "conversion" theory this way: "On the basis of our experience—the embarrassment, shame and humiliation so many of us have known—we would definitely advise anyone who has not yet become an active homosexual, but has only misgivings about himself, to go the other way, if he can."*

Speaking for myself, I don't know of any young person who was ever "converted" to homosexuality, but I'm rather well acquainted with at least one little girl who adores her lesbian sister and has had four years of periodically intensive contact with her and many of her friends. We've all watched

---

* Quoted in John J. McNeill, *The Church and the Homosexual* (Mission, Kans.: Sheed Andrews & McMeel, Inc., 1976), p. 160.

Abby growing up "blatantly heterosexual" as Avril once described her. There couldn't be a better example of a child fulfilling her own promise regardless of outside influences, especially since all of us in her family accept homosexuality as a natural phenomenon.

A good example occurred recently. Matt had a new girl friend who was becoming something of a fixture around our house, and Abby, who loves romance better than anything, was delighted. "Matt likes her a lot," she announced to me one day in the kitchen. "They hug and kiss! It's so romantic!" I asked her, "Don't you think it's romantic when Avril and her girl friends hug and kiss?" Actually I knew what she would say, but I wanted to hear it in her own words. Abby, who didn't know she would be quoted for publication, thought seriously about her answer. "Well, not in the way we've been brought up to believe. It's not the same thing as Vivien Leigh and Clark Gable. I can relate more to Matt and May."

We had never meant to discuss Avril's lesbianism with all our relatives, but the more deeply I became involved with speaking, writing, organizational work, and such, the harder it became to hide. I have never been comfortable making up stories, and when people ask me what I'm doing these days I generally think, Here it comes, and tell them.

Recently some rather distant Roman Catholic relatives visited our family on a day when my husband was out of town. They asked how the new book was coming. I gulped and said rather stupidly, "You mean Mother told you about the new book?" My twelve-year-old cleared her throat and pointedly left the table, indicating by wild gyrations of the eyes and eyebrows that she wanted no part of the brouhaha that was certainly coming. My relatives said of course they had heard about the book—why should my mother not have told them about it? I blundered on, saying that I supposed they might be offended, and explained my interest in writing for parents of gays. At which point my aunt said, "Oh, you mean you're writing a book on your own now?" It turned out that the last they knew I was doing some science writing with my husband—I had made my own trap and jumped right into the middle of it.

But they were nice and told me they had always noticed Avril's lack of interest in men. Abby returned, consumed by curiosity, and I explained that she had left fearing an argument. "Oh no, not in these days," said my aunt. "Thirty years ago we would have certainly been shocked, but today it's even on television and everybody knows all about it."

I don't know what people may be saying about our family behind our backs, and I've learned not to worry about it. The point is, if friends and relatives care enough about having us in their lives, they'll accept all of us as we are. If not, it's their loss. We have each other. If my husband and I expect our children to stand behind us, we have to set the example by trusting their judgment and backing up their own decisions. And it's been my experience that when I come on strong and tell it the way I see it I get a better response than I would by pussyfooting around the issue. Most people are reluctant to confront a mother who is basically daring them to attack her young.

I recently wrote about my activities to my father's eldest sister, eighty-four, since she lives in Canada and we don't see each other often. This is what she wrote back: "I hope the book you and your Denver friend are writing is developing well. There must be a great need for better understanding and sympathy for Nature's Variation on a Theme."

We've never read or heard any statement that went to the heart of the matter with such grace and simplicity. Every man and woman alive represents a set of variations—people are not mass-produced like cars or robots. There is no one single set of characteristics that can be labeled "normal." Psychologists tell us that if you can hold a job, get along with neighbors and associates, build a network of friendships, and maintain loving relationships, you are functioning normally. We know literally thousands of gay people from every walk of life, many of whom are assumed by family and casual friends to be completely straight because they seem so "normal."

Sure, there are some disturbed and neurotic homosexuals. Any movement based on tolerance for anomalous behavior, as the gay rights movement is, attracts a certain number of individuals who have had difficulty being accepted by peers. Religious communities, for example, can often attract their own share of outcasts. That doesn't mean that the whole group is made up of them.

We think that knowing and working with gays has made us better people. We've been accepted into gay communities. We've met trust and ready friendship there, and we've learned to function as members of a minority group existing in a majority culture, a new experience for both of us. Our lives have been immeasurably enriched through our experiences, as we have come to know many interesting and beautiful people, to examine and discard our own outmoded attitudes, and to see the world from a different stance.

Eventually, each of us joined the growing Parents of Gays movement (see Chapter 9), in which parents work together to gain a positive perspective toward homosexuality and to renew and deepen family ties.

Betty says:

My real education about homosexuality and its impact on the family began when I started to work with Parents of Gays. When word got around to various gay organizations and individuals that I was planning to start a parents' group —first in Washington, D.C., and later in Denver—I began to hear from far more troubled gay women and men than from parents. I soon found that they, too, needed to understand what their parents were going through, and that for our gay children, rejection by their parents, or the fear of such rejection, is a primary concern. But countless subsequent conversations and much correspondence with parents revealed to me the various and common anxieties most of us experience. And so one of our main themes as we talk with parents is the vital importance of our continuing love and support, as well as understanding, of our gay children.

Over the years we have talked with, or heard from, scores of parents—people like you and like us all, from all parts of the country. And it is probably clear by now that we two make no claim to be *the* experts, the *only* parents who understand our children—far from it. Across the country many, many mothers and fathers are dealing with this same experience: learning, loving, reaching out, growing. Their individual experiences are as important as any we have had; their contributions, along with those of our gay friends and acquaintances, are integral to what we say in this book and elsewhere. For they, too, are working in various and often unsung ways to bring families together again and to right some of the wrongs that gay women and men have suffered for all too many years.

What is clear to us is that, within families, there is no longer any need for fear, for accusations, for terrible secrets. If the closet is out-of-date for our children, it is certainly out-of-date for us, and there is no reason for us to remain in its dark and lonely interior. The key to opening the door of this closet is nothing more or less than an open mind. Without that key, we shall never leave it. With it, we cannot help but emerge into the light.

And so we warn you that this book will challenge you. We will set forth concepts you may never have considered before. We will argue, with some backup information, against old "beliefs" and "rules." And we will open new vistas for those who seek them.

We're going to talk a lot about homosexuality (surprise!), and about what being lesbian or gay means to women and men who so identify themselves (or are so identified by others). We'll be talking more about the myths, the misconceptions, and the stereotypes—which never have been true for most gay people, and which must be discarded from our thinking as useless and harmful baggage.

You will be hearing many firsthand stories in the words that gay people and their parents have written or spoken to each other and to us. You will see how families work through to understanding and how, in some cases, others have not yet done so. We'll discuss the common problems that face both parent and child, along with some of the solutions. The information you'll find here, which is based on our personal experience and on scientific research and other authoritative sources, will provide answers to many of your questions.

You will get an inside look at the lives of different gay people (and will find them to be of the same variety and complexity as nongays' lives); you'll learn what unique problems gay people do face (and that most of them can be attributed to a homophobic society rather than to their sexual orientation), and you'll discover what forces for change are currently at work.

We'll talk about gay couples and gays who are heterosexually married, about child custody for lesbian and gay male parents. We provide an approach to religious objections, along with views from psychologists and the results of studies—and all the other things you've always wanted to know about this variation of sexuality but were afraid to even think about! You'll find annotated lists of books to read and additional helpful material and sources of information.

And we hope that as we set off on this venture together, you will find warmth and caring and a new understanding of "the love that dared not speak its name"—and a wealth of good and exciting experiences that will change your life.

The Children's Story

I tried to explain it in the best way that I knew,
But you just closed your eyes,
You didn't want to hear it.

And I didn't want to hurt you
And I didn't want to have to go,
But I felt you didn't know me,
And I had to let you know....

—LYNN COOK

One of the ways we human beings learn about each other is simply by listening to what others are saying. Yet no matter how sincerely we listen to other people, we sometimes fail to do this with our own children.

When our sons and daughters speak to us of themselves, sharing deeply personal feelings, we must look beyond their immediate words to discover the totality of their message. Let us examine what it means to our children to tell us they are gay. What has brought about their decision to share this with us? Why, in fact, do they have to tell us? Or are we too engrossed in our own feelings to consider the process that led to our daughter's declaration? Do we want to believe that our son has told us this news thoughtlessly, perhaps because for some reason he wants to "shake us up"? (Doesn't he *know* how much this will upset us?)

As a matter of fact, how the family will take the news is a subject of intense interest to most gay people. Take any group of lesbians and/or gay men, add one parent who is comfortable talking with them, and sooner or later the conversation centers around the subject of parents.

"How can I tell my parents so they won't be upset?" they ask us.

"*Should* I tell my folks? I'm afraid they'll never understand."

"My Mom is having a lot of trouble with this. She's really unhappy, and nothing I say seems to do any good."

"My Dad won't even talk about it. What can I do?"

They want to know about parents, too.

"How did you and your husband react when your daughter told you?"

"How did you actually feel when you found out your son was gay? What did you say to him?"

"How long did it take you to get over feeling bad about having a gay child? Or did you ever feel bad?"

And they share their own experiences with each other.

"Let me tell you what happened when *I* broke the news!"

"How come *your* parents took it so well—and mine haven't?"

"I came out even before you did, but I still haven't been able to tell my folks."

In trying to understand what it means to our children to "tell us," we must first discover what precedes the telling; the announcement itself is likely to be a more or less final step in a long process. By the time a young girl confides in her parents, she usually has done a great deal of soul-searching, sometimes painfully, first of all simply to acknowledge that she is lesbian. A considerable amount of stress may likewise accompany a young man's awareness that he will never "like girls" (as sexual partners, at any rate), and that, by nature, he is attracted to other men.

Most of our gay young people grow up in a society that abhors and persecutes the very kind of persons they know themselves to be. Therefore, rather than agonize over the "tragedy" that has befallen *us* as parents, we might better try to discover what our gay child has experienced in earlier years. What do we know of how it feels to grow up gay? Or do we assume that our child has only now "decided" (or been "persuaded") to be gay? Do we believe what our child is telling us? In one book written for parents, *Now What?*, Bill Hutchinson* tells a couple of true stories about the latter question: " 'My mother looked me straight in the eye and listened while I explained everything to her,' recalled a lesbian in her late 20s, 'and then she said, "I don't believe you and I don't want to hear another word about it." ' "

The second story is similar: a young man whose parents made no response to his announcement, except his mother asked him not to bring up the subject again and said she felt he would "outgrow it." The young man says, "My God, I'm almost thirty years old. I've been gay for twelve years. Why won't they listen to what I'm saying?"

If we truly want to understand our children, we must stop *explaining* them to themselves and listen to what they have to say to us.

Jeff Moses, who had recently told his mother of his gayness, wrote this to her:

Look at this for a moment from the perspective of the gay child. (Yes, there are gay children: Ned knew he was gay from the time he was in sixth grade; I knew there was something "wrong" from the time I hit junior high. We are not atypical.) The gay child sees *no* healthy gay people, as such. He/she hears the locker room humor, reads about "homosexual murderers" in the paper (did you ever see a reference to a heterosexual

---

* See Bibliography for details about availability.

murderer?), sees the limp-wristed stereotypes in the movies and on TV. If a child is gay, he/she usually has no healthy role models to turn to. George Q. was the first reasonably healthy gay person I ever met. He was not the *first* gay person I'd met; if I'd patterned my relationships after the ones I'd seen before, I'd be a mess. Gay kids need to know that they can be gay and healthy. Denying them access to healthy gay role models is a little like denying contraceptives to people under 16 "so they won't get pregnant." ...

I lived in the closet for years; I know a lot of people who are still in the closet. It's HELL. Imagine a world where you and Walter had to hide not only your relationship but even the possibility of your relationship. Imagine not being able to hold hands in a public place for fear you'd be told you had to move out of your apartment. Imagine having to pretend you hardly knew each other when your children came to visit, or your friends, for fear you'd be charged with "lewd sexual conduct" and fired from your job. Imagine hearing your friends talk openly about their love and not being able to say a word about yours. Imagine having to go to a "swingers' bar" because that's the only place you could find someone to be intimate with. Imagine being told you weren't fit to be in the company of children without supervision. Imagine walking down the street and being yelled at by people in passing cars calling out obscenities. Imagine being blackmailed, beaten up in alleys, even brutally murdered. That's what it's like in the closet; that's why I came out; that's why I want to help other people come out. ... I'm not asking society to stamp me "good." I'm asking society to stop branding me "evil." There's a huge difference.

According to gay people, both women and men, many of them knew from a very early age (even at three or four or five years) that they were "different." They didn't have words for it; none could say at that tender age, "I am homosexual," but they sensed that somehow they did not fit the picture of what girls or boys were "supposed to be." Many have experienced an attraction to others of the same gender for most of their lives. For example, women tell us that they *always* "noticed" pictures of other women more than those of men; the same is true in reverse of males. Betty recalls that Glenn said he had "known what he was" since junior high school. "He once told me that he had resented the fact that I was totally unaware of what he was 'going through' at the time, although he acknowledges that he had deliberately hidden from me any clues to his feelings of distress or confusion." Avril tells Nancy now that she was miserable for years and hid it. She never even knew why, or how, only that it was something she had to bear alone.

While some gay people recall that as emerging sexual persons their gayness was never a problem, that they accepted "where it was at" for them right from the beginning, probably a greater number have struggled with, or repressed, what for them are natural feelings, as a seemingly unavoidable concession to society. For the latter, their acknowledgment of their own sexual orientation has been a long and painful journey with no outside support of any kind. Even after this inner knowledge is clear, it may take some time for women and men to feel good about themselves. Usually, however, once a gay woman begins to meet and know other lesbians (which doesn't always happen as soon as she knows she is lesbian), her feelings of self-worth grow to the point where she is finally free of pretense and fear. And sooner or later these young people want to share this part of themselves with their parents. Obviously, no one can encompass the scope of several years' experience in a single disclosure, no matter how well-chosen and positive the words. That is why we as parents must listen to our gay children beyond their initial declaration. It is instructive to learn that what Jeff Moses wrote to his mother (above) made a vital change in her. His mother, Lucille, told us:

It was not until Jeff wrote me the letter that a flood of understanding came. I wept over that letter. I could see what he had had to face in his junior high years and I felt terrible that I had not known and given him my understanding and love. That letter did it. My understanding came while reading it—almost in shock waves. Everything he wrote was rational to me. In other words, I had never really thought about what it must be like to be gay. The part about the gay child never seeing any healthy gay people (and other things he said) really penetrated. . . . My heart ached for my son and other gays.

A low self-image is one of the hardest things for gay people to deal with as they mature. While the growth of supportive gay communities, especially in larger cities, is making it easier for women and men to acknowledge that they are gay and to feel good about themselves, there are still thousands of gay people who have internalized society's views of homosexuality and who therefore, at least at first, act in the only ways they know to be "gay." Jake, from Kansas, was one of these.

At twenty-one, Jake hated himself for what he was and felt at various times dirty, insane, and perverted. Resorting to drugs and alcohol to hide his self-hatred, he also frequented gay bars; there he found companions who were into cosmetics and "drag." This, to him, was what being gay was. He confesses that his own subsequent street behavior was "outrageous." Eventually the police confirmed this belief by arresting him, and that night his parents were introduced to Jake's sexual orientation. The police called his father, who came and took him home. But although both parents tried their best to help their son with love and concern, Jake continued to go the drug-and-drink route and was thoroughly unhappy. Somewhere along the way he transferred his feelings about himself to the entire gay community, blaming others for his misery. About six months later he left home and arrived in Los Angeles a bitter and angry young man.

Here, as he began to meet a different kind of gay person, Jake gradually gave up his outward affectations of effeminacy, but his inner turmoil continued. Eventually he began to work with the Gay Community Services Center among young men and women who clearly accepted themselves and who genuinely seemed to care about him. And soon, as he was no longer hating himself, he stopped blaming others for his unhappy state. He "came out" all over again, into a new world of stability and self-acceptance. Jake's one overriding regret is that he gave his parents such a wretched and negative picture of what being gay is, and he hopes to be able to change that view.

As good healthy role models emerge—as more stable, articulate, and respected gay people come out openly—some of the appearances and forms of behavior that have been unwittingly copied by young men and women disappear, and with them much of the anguish of self-denigration and self-hate.

When we begin to perceive what our children have experienced—perhaps over a long period of time and with a range of internal feelings—before coming to terms with their own sexual orientation, it is clear that their decision to tell us has not been lightly made. But some of us wonder *why* they tell us. We may wish at first that we didn't have to know this about our child. Yet there are many good reasons why young men and women want to, or feel they must, share this part of their lives with Mom and Dad.

In the first place, while being gay is not the *only* thing there is to know about a person (although some of us act as if it were), it is an important and necessary part of that person's life. "But," we have heard parents protest, "our straight children don't tell us about their sex lives." The reality is that our *gay* children are not telling us about their sex lives—what they do in the bedroom—but about their innate feelings, and how those feelings affect their lives, their friendships, and the choice of people they love. When our daughter comes home and says she's met a really nice man, we are usually interested and happy for her. But we are not likely to greet our son so positively if he happens to mention *he* has met a "really nice man"—if we are not aware that he is gay. Young gay women and men, in order to share the joys and events and concerns of their lives, must tell their parents this fact about themselves.

Unfortunately, as Jeff indicated in his letter, too many gay people are still forced to spend a lot of energy hiding the very events and relationships they would like to share. One young man told us how much he wished he had been able to tell his parents that a few months before, when he was very disturbed and unhappy after his lover had left him, he had rather desperately needed the comfort and understanding of his parents. But he could not ask for it, as they knew nothing of this part of his life. "If it had been a girl who left me," he said, "they would have been right there for me. But as it was, I went through a very difficult time, and yet had to act as if nothing were wrong."

Furthermore, keeping this part of one's life hidden, for whatever reasons, is bound to create a barrier between child and parent—even if Mom and Dad don't know it. There's so much that can't be said, and very often questions that simply cannot be answered.

"When are you going to bring home a nice girl?" "What *are* these activities you mention in your letters?" "Isn't there someone special in your life?" Although the answer to the last question may well be affirmative, how is a son or daughter to respond if the folks don't *know?*

Frequently the young person's living situation has to be more or less concealed from parents who aren't aware that their child is gay. When a gay couple live together, the prospect of a visit from parents can cause considerable panic. We know of gay couples who have two bedrooms, the second of which they use only when Mom and Dad are around. This kind of deception and all the peripheral aspects of it (no displays of affection, friends forbidden to call during the visit) make for a less than open, warm meeting with the parents.

In still another situation—the breakup of a marriage in

which husband or wife is gay—telling the parents (perhaps both sets) is often a necessity to explain "what happened." None of this need be traumatic, of course, when we parents know and understand our gay children and are as comfortable with them as we are with our nongay children and their partners.

In any case, these are some of the reasons why our children decide to share their gayness with us. Naturally, how they do this varies from person to person, from family to family. If they can, most gay people try to tell their parents (or perhaps only one of them) face-to-face during a carefully planned weekend at home or a conversation after dinner or a long ride in the country. Sometimes, however, the news comes out in an unforeseen way. If the child is living at home, perhaps still in school, parents may begin to wonder about their son's frequent phone calls from other guys, or about their daughter's relationship with a particular woman. They may start to ask questions (or, unfortunately, to make accusations) that bring out the truth. Occasionally, parents come upon their son or daughter in an embrace with someone of the same sex. Sometimes, when parent and child are living apart, a telephone call will provide the revelation. And quite often the postman will deliver a fat envelope containing unexpected news.

While many gay people feel face-to-face is better so they can answer their parents' questions on the spot, others decide that a phone call, perhaps preceding a visit, will set the scene for later discussion without undue emotional response at the time. And still others would rather write the carefully worded letter which their parents can read (perhaps several times) without having to respond immediately to their child. We cannot say which is the *best* way; so much depends on already established relationships and ways of communicating within the family. Although it is far better for gay children to talk with Mom and Dad only after they feel comfortable with their sexuality, this is not always possible, and it is up to parents to deal with the situation as helpfully as possible.

Here's how some gay men and women handled their approach:

Lou wrote a long letter to his parents, intending to leave it with them after an upcoming visit home when he would tell them he was gay. He looked forward to a good discussion with them, feeling that they would have little trouble accepting his homosexuality. He believed that this letter, which he had worked on carefully (and from which we give only excerpts) would tie up the loose ends and reinforce the information that he would share in person with his parents.

Dear Mom and Dad:

By the time you read this I will have told you that I'm a homosexual. I know this must be a difficult situation for you. Undoubtedly all kinds of negative thoughts are running through your minds. Will our son be happy? Why is he "different"? What will relatives and neighbors think?

There are many who have advised me never to tell my parents I'm gay. "Why create problems and tensions, and maybe even lose the love of your parents forever?" they ask.

I think it's to your credit that I can't do this. I just can't, and won't, live a lie! What's more, I deeply believe it would be an insult to you had I concluded that you were incapable of looking beyond the generations of erroneous information, slander, and downright silliness that have molded the prevailing opinion of homosexuals. It's not easy to brush aside the horrible myths you've been told about homosexuals—especially when they have been perpetuated by "experts." But I truly believe that once you have made an honest and sincere attempt to examine the situation objectively, you will come to view homosexuality as being just as healthy and natural as heterosexuality, and as just another variation in human sexuality and love.

In the meantime, how will we relate to each other?

I wish I could honestly answer that question. I can only say that I'm through pretending. The cat is out of the bag. When you ask me what I've been doing, or what's new, I'm going to tell you. (That is, if you decide to ask. And I hope you do.). . .

For as long as I can remember I have been more sexually attracted to men than to women; however, I do *not* dislike women. While living at home, I haven't "gone out with girls," as you know. But I have gone out with women while at college and in Washington. I believe the strong societal taboos on homosexuality, combined with my hectic activities over the past number of years (college, extracurricular activities, hobbies, graduate school/part-time work, etc.), kept my mind off the question of "where my head was at."

Another factor was involved. Before investigating the matter, my only conception of gay people was what society had instilled in me (and which I'm afraid may be instilled in you). This was the image of the stereotype "faggot" with limp wrists, flamboyant clothing, and lisp. The average gay person, I believed, was mostly confined to the fields of theater, interior decorating, and hairdressing. He certainly hated sports, and invariably was effeminate and "bitchy."

I'm about as close to that description as a tiger is to a tadpole. So, therefore, I can't be gay, I told myself. For a while.

After finishing school and starting on a job with regular working hours, I finally began to explore the part of me I had ignored for so long. I began reading up on the subject. Finally, it was time to act. . . . I got in touch with a gay counseling center and found out where to go to meet people; the counselor also warned me of some of the pitfalls (related to "society's reaction").

I've come a long way since then. Yet I'm still in a period of adjustment. But if you understand the expression "it fits like a glove," you will understand how I feel today.

As it turned out, Lou's parents did not accept his news calmly, as he had expected, but were extremely upset. Lou was devastated by their unyielding negative attitude. When he talked to us about it, we encouraged him not to give up hope, but to allow his mother and father time to absorb his news.

During the next few months his mother continued to urge Lou to get psychiatric help to "change" (which he refused to do), while his father repeatedly warned that "if this ever got out," it would ruin his son's career. Both parents (unaware that Lou's brother and sister already knew) insisted that he speak of this to *none* of his relatives. As time passed, Lou realized that his parents' attitudes were beginning to change; they would sometimes comment on gay-related issues covered on TV, and as more gay news was made public, they seemed to feel less isolated in dealing with the matter. By the summer of 1977 they were much freer in discussing the subject and asking questions. Lou says he now talks freely with his parents about his life and that they deal comfortably with the friends he occasionally takes home to visit.

Barbara Griffith, now in her early thirties, talked with her parents about her gayness several years ago, and also told her brother and sister. At one point her brother wrote her a long letter full of questions and comments. In her response, Barbara answers the points her brother raised, and in so doing speaks for herself as a lesbian.

Dear Vic,
Thanks for the honesty and frankness with which you related your feelings on my being a lesbian. As you might guess, we have some basic points of disagreement, such as your belief that homosexuality is a "deviation from biological form" and "arrested sexual development." The only way I can see that it deviates from biological form is as far as procreation is concerned, and I don't think that simply because Tab A in Slot B works best for producing human beings, it's enough reason for imposing limitations. There's no question but that it's contrary to *social custom,* but I came to believe pretty early that "social custom" was a questionable criterion on which to base my personal beliefs, feelings, actions, etc.
As for its being a "choice," I am a person whose primary

orientation and preference is toward other women; therefore, I *am* a lesbian. My *choice,* as I see it, is in whether to be honest about my feelings or to continue to deny/hide them, based on definitions imposed by others. I told you about going to the library when I was in high school and rejecting what I read about lesbianism as applicable to me personally. At the same time, though, I decided on a surface level that there was nothing inherently wrong with homosexuality, "it's just not for me." The latter came more from a rejection of the definitions than from a rejection of my feeling, and from the fear that the definitions instill. That was ten years ago.

The first five or so years after that, I didn't even question the definitions—just tried to live in the prescribed roles. But my strongest attachments and deepest feelings continued to be directed to women.

About that time, an extremely deep friendship I had with another woman fell apart with a lot of pain. For the next four years I carried around a lot of guilt for the falling apart, because in the last stages of the relationship I did some pretty strange, uncharacteristic things, like getting extremely jealous, possessive, etc. I took on the blame for the relationship's disintegration until I realized where my actions had been coming from— the fact that I was very much in love with her, but so damned scared of the idea that I couldn't talk about it, much less act on it. When that realization hit me, I decided that I could never again let myself get so hung up on a fear that I'd deny the honesty of my feelings. That was the point of liberation, and I've moved from there to where I am now. . . .

Why tell my family? I'm beginning to wonder if I haven't been speaking in a vacuum, since none of you has been able to hear what I'm saying—*I'm happy.* I feel like a whole person for the first time ever. And I wanted to share that celebration with you. Because the world is so slow to change, it's going to be a while before I'll be able to be completely open, but in the interim I'm going to be as open as I can with as many people as I can. After the past ten years' struggle to resolve it, I'm sharing (or *trying* to share) the peace and happiness that the resolution has brought. . . .

I hope this answers some of your questions, and I hope you'll feel free to ask more as they arise. You're right, this is something I'm pretty open about—the more open *more* of us can be, the more chance I'll have of seeing the world be liberated from its prejudices, perhaps even in my lifetime.

Mitch, a Californian, is twenty-five and the youngest of four children.

I came to the harsh realization that I was gay when I was fifteen and in the ninth grade. One afternoon I went into the boys' gym to deliver the school newspaper—and it hit me like a hammer on the head: I liked guys in the way I was supposed to like girls!

As I looked back it got clearer, and I could remember things that foreshadowed this. But everything I had experienced to that point I had assumed *every* guy felt. I did not realize I was "different."

Face it—in America, you just aren't supposed to be different. So I went through high school enjoying things as best I could, never daring to tell anyone my secret. I dated, but I never had the desire to be sexual with a girl.

Once in college, I no longer felt the peer pressure to put up a false front, so basically I quit dating. I soon found I hated school, and my anxiety was skyrocketing; I flunked out in June 1971....

I began to make some new friends. About ten of us, mostly heterosexual, became very close to each other, and that meant a lot to me; surprisingly, no one ever asked me about my lack of girl friends.

Then, in 1973, I heard about *The Advocate,* a gay newspaper. (A gay newspaper! I couldn't believe it.) Within a week, in Hollywood with friends to see a movie, I saw my first copy of it on a corner newsstand. I cried inside because I was with four straight macho males who would kill me if they knew I was gay.... Later, I drove back to Hollywood alone and bought a copy. A whole new world was opened: there were gay people out there! Soon I was buying every issue, but I still had never met another gay person.

In early 1974, I moved into an apartment with my friend

Larry and a friend of his, Dennis. Dennis and I hit it off and became good friends. When Larry got married a year later, Dennis and I decided to move into a smaller apartment. During this whole time, my anxiety about my homosexuality was surfacing and I knew that before Dennis and I moved, I should tell him I was gay and let him know what I was going through.

His reaction was immediate—shock—but his verbal response was superior: "Mitch, you're still my friend and your telling me this brings us closer together." I still consider Dennis my best friend, although we don't see much of each other.

From that point on, I knew I would have to deal with my sexuality. The only way I knew to do this at the time was through *The Advocate*. I searched for an ad that was not just a sex ad. In late October I found one and wrote an answer. I received a phone number in response. After countless times of dialing and hanging up, I let his phone ring, and Mark answered. We talked and talked. In fact, we talked on the phone for a month before I had the courage to meet him. I had told myself that it would be a far-off chance if we liked each other—but we did.

I told my brother first. "I'm gay." He was silent. After a minute or so we began to talk. I expressed my fears that everyone in the family knew I was gay. He said no, no one had brought it up. His first question, curiously enough, was: "How long have you known?"

Mark and I saw each other till about March 1976, when our relationship ended. During that time and later, I got very depressed. I realized I did not like Mark emotionally. I did not like his friends. I did not like the "gay scene." So I retreated to my "closet." For some time I contemplated suicide.

Then, on Memorial Day, 1976, I was very upset because I was supposed to go to my sister's for a family get-together. These holiday gatherings *always* reinforced my loneliness. But early that day I happened to buy a copy of *NewsWest* (another gay paper), and I noticed two items about gay rap groups. As it happened, neither was open (it was a holiday). But I went on to the family party, surprisingly happy.

The next day I called again and found that the Gay Community Center raps were on Thursday evenings; fifteen to thirty

people show up; I wouldn't have to talk if I didn't want to. . . .
Far out. I went to my first rap. *Four* people. I was scared shit-
less. But I soon started talking, and it was three months before
I stopped.

In July I told my parents. I had prepared myself to accept
being disowned, but that did not happen. It was almost too easy.
They took it hard, but maturely. This is how it went:

By this time, I was going to the Gay Community Center at
least twice a week, and getting involved. Although I didn't live
at home, we're a close family, and everyone had been asking
where I was all the time. So this one evening I was finally alone
with my parents.

I told them.

After the initial shock, we talked for two hours. They wanted
to get me help, which I said I didn't need. They weren't truly
convinced I was gay. (I'm not sure they are yet. . . . It's been
close to a year, and I'm now finding that it's an undiscussed
subject that I'm going to have to shed more light on. By not
talking about it, my Mom has allowed herself delusions about
my homosexuality, i.e., that I could be straight if I wanted to.)

Mitch says that he's now heavily involved with the Gay
Community Center. He is not sexually promiscuous and is
hoping to find a lover. He's very vocal about homosexuality,
writes signed letters to the editor, and gives talks on homosexuality at classes. He says, "I'm very comfortable about
being gay. There's no sin as I see it. I hurt no one and live
a good productive life." One of his goals is to "make the
general public aware of gays, and of what homosexuality is
all about."

Coming out some twenty-four years ago was a different
kind of experience for Joe Jenkins. Joe was born in San
Francisco, spent many of his formative years in the Midwest, and currently lives in California, where he, his lover
of some twelve years, and another longtime friend are re-
storing a historically designated Victorian home. Joe writes:

I was twenty-three years old when my parents found out that I was gay. I would rather have died than have my parents know, and I saw no reason for them to know, since I knew it would hurt them. I gave little thought to the hurt it was causing me, as I felt that it was my cross to bear. A mistake. Just the strain of living a lie (even though they didn't know I was "lying") was very heavy for me, as we had always been a very close family. What it really broke down to was that I didn't want to hurt my mother and the very idea of my father's finding out was terrifying.

It was winter and I had written a letter to a friend telling him that I had fallen in love. The letter itself was prefaced by a poem of A. E. Housman's. One day, while cleaning my room, my mother ran across the poem and read it, thinking it might have been one of those I was writing in those days. She read one page and continued onto the second when she discovered she was no longer reading poetry but my confession of love for another man. (I never condemned her for this, as she was not prying—and the discovery was a mistake.) She called my father.

He and I were at work. He came over to me and said that we were leaving for home. He looked kind of grave, but I had no hint of what was to come—I was just glad we were going home. In the car he asked me directly, "Are you a queer?" I said, "Why do you ask?" He said, "Because your mother read a letter and . . ." I interrupted with: "The answer is yes." The words were flat and completely devoid of emotion. I felt nothing but a heavy sensation in my chest . . . no relief at letting out my long-suppressed secret . . . no fear of reproach . . . nothing. As I recall, nothing further was said during what seemed like an unending drive home.

We all assembled in the kitchen, but I cannot recall much of the talk that followed. It was an unpleasant, tense experience for all of us. I was horrified to see my mother's head bobbing with a nervous tic. My father, always stern-looking, appeared even more so and, furthermore, he looked hopeless and floundering, as he did not know how to cope with the situation.

Then, even though I was twenty-three, I was grounded. I was not to go out on weekends or see any of the people I had been seeing (even though they knew nothing of these people). For reasons I must have thought would work at the time, I accepted these terms. . . .

Life went on. Because we were still close, things gradually reached a point where we could talk. I recall telling my parents about other gay people I knew that they also knew (but didn't realize were gay): the couple that ran my father's favorite restaurant . . . a boy working for my father of whom he was very fond . . . customers of his. I explained as best I could about the gay trip—not very well, I'm afraid, as it was still new to me, too, and not very rewarding in many ways. I was lonely, and I had already been through a puppy love thing that tore me apart emotionally.

Finally, by asking permission to go out and gradually letting them know I was not out raping the state, the matter became less prominent at table and I kind of resumed my normal activities. I brought friends home for them to meet, and they liked some of them. Soon they realized that in all respects save for the time I was not around them I was the same person I had always been. The ice had been broken . . . and all of us had survived.

Dave Cassidy was very active in gay community affairs in Toronto, and when he later moved to Montreal to join his lover, he became similarly deeply involved in that city. Among many other projects, Dave organized the first Parents of Gays group in Canada (bilingual: "Nous adorons aussi nos enfants gais"). In mid-1977, Dave and a friend, John Blacklock, taped their own personal stories for this book. First, Dave's account:

I told my mother and father in early August 1974. They were the last people I had to tell, and I decided it would be a good idea to do so, to bring us closer. I wrote a long letter and sent along a copy of *Society and the Healthy Homosexual*. I later found out from my mother that she would have liked a more direct approach—face-to-face, that is—rather than this indirect approach. But I had to prepare myself, so I thought, for the eventuality that there would be a complete break between us. So in the letter I suggested a meeting together to talk about it.

Now That You Know

Their first reactions were rather typical. My mother's was that she had done something to "cause" me to be this way. My father's reaction was based on his recollection of a couple of persons he had worked with when he was younger who were, as he called them, "chicken-hawks" [men who are attracted to much younger men]. Therefore, with only that reference point, in his mind *I* had to be a chicken-hawk. So I decided that there had to be a long period of educational effort.... Otherwise, they seemed to feel it was fine for me to live my own life-style, as long as I didn't flaunt it or tell anybody else about it. Of course I told my brother and sister. My brother is a psychiatrist who had no qualms one way or the other, and my sister was extremely positive and still is. I've grown much closer to them since then.

A few weeks ago I asked my mother to write her story, to contribute to this book. This was the straw that broke the camel's back; it brought along a lot more anguish. Just a week ago I received a letter from her saying she was all in tears and would rather not be reminded of anything that had to do with this particular aspect of my life. All I can say now is that my rather subtle efforts during the last three years on an educational level have not, in my opinion, worked. I have even wondered if it was worth all the anguish and the effort I went through to tell them.... I'm now about to write them a letter and tell them more or less to get it together, that a relationship is a two-way street, and they've caused me a lot of hurt—a fact I don't think they've ever tried to deal with....

I was at home recently, after an absence of about thirteen months, for about four or five days. Not *once* while I was there did the conversation turn to *my* life, nor was my lover's name mentioned except as I was leaving, as sort of an afterthought. So that reinforced my perception of their wish to hide it all. I suppose I should have taken the bull by the horns more, but I try to take the subtle approach and let things work out without pressuring. But perhaps a little more pressure is needed....

It wasn't until I met Walter that I began to know what I wanted for the rest of my life—and then I proceeded, through a long course of pure hell, to get what I wanted. And during that long course of pure hell, my parents were of absolutely no help. There was really only one person, a gay person, to whom I could, and did, turn for help—for solace and conversation, for airing my thoughts.

And that situation exists right up to the present time; I can count on one hand the people that I turn to. And my parents are not numbered in that group. I still don't feel I can sit down and talk to them and get any sort of understanding. And I wonder—people tell me I should work at getting a better understanding—but I still wonder if it's worth all the tediousness and effort. But I suppose I'll continue a while longer, since part of me doesn't want to give up on the idea of having a close relationship with my parents. Especially since I went through all that crap to get this far. . . . Even then, it hasn't worked . . . yet.

John Blacklock (aged thirty-seven):

I remember very clearly the circumstances under which I first let my parents know that I was gay. I was thirty at the time, and I had been living away from home from the time I was twenty years old—at school, and later at work as a teacher—and I'd been visiting home at Christmas and part of every summer. And, by the way, I'm my parents' only child.

It was a few weeks before I was due to go home for Christmas holidays during my thirtieth year. I'd spent a few weeks beforehand in preparation; the psychological pressure to let my parents in on the very exciting things that had been happening to me had been building up for the last year or so, and I went over and formulated and made up sentences in my mind—to break it to them over the telephone. I wanted to tell them so they would have a few weeks to think it over before they actually saw me in person. I can't remember my exact words on the telephone—it was my mother I was talking to—but I don't think I came up with the smooth, polished phrases I intended to; I think I rather blurted it out. My mother, I think, came up with the reaction she probably thought she was expected to— this is *terrible,* she'd never *thought* of anything like that, she never wanted to see me again, she wished *I* was dead, she wished *she* was dead, et cetera, et cetera. . . . It was quite a scene for the entire phone conversation.

About four days later she called me again and confessed that actually she'd suspected for years and that it hadn't been any big surprise to her. She'd been thinking it over, and she wanted to try to understand—and no, she was glad she was alive, she was glad I was alive, and yes, she did want to see me again at Christmas.

When I did go home that Christmas, and during the years since then, my father, who was a beautiful and very gentle person, was, as far as I can tell, immediately and totally accepting. And there was never, up to his death, any change in the very fine relationship we'd always had.

With Mother it's been somewhat more difficult. I think that over a period of a year or two she came to accept the idea of putting one more adjective to the description of her son, and at least to be willing to accept that son as she always had, without fully understanding what the adjective meant. Because I rarely visit my parents, and they never come to visit me, they experience their son as a person who *calls* himself gay, but they've never had the chance to see me living, loving, interacting with other people who are gay; so that my gay life, as opposed to myself as a gay person, has never been a reality for them. If I wished for anything, it would be that my mother could experience some of that. I think it would only be when she had actually experienced and understood the reality of my total life, as opposed simply to my being someone who identifies himself in a particular way, that she would achieve real acceptance and understanding.

Right now, perhaps we can turn to our own daughter who is lesbian, or to our gay son, and say, "I think I know a little of how it has been for you. I need to know a lot more. Tell me. I promise I will listen to what you have to say."

The Parents' Story

Sarah Montgomery has told her tale many times. Since
September 1972, when she got the news that her forty-six-
year-old son and his lover had committed suicide, her story
has become almost a classic among gay people, and for
many others too. And yet, beyond its personal tragedy, its
sense of terrible loss, hers is a story of love and courage
and hope.

Sarah, a lifelong feminist, became an active suffragette at
sixteen. Now, at seventy-nine, "her voice is undimmed in its
clarity and energy"* as she continues to speak to the needs
and rights of gay people everywhere.

As her son Charlie was growing up, composing and loving music, his mother knew that he battled against the epi-
thet *fairy*. She taught him how to fight back. ("Tear their

---

* All quotations in this story are from "Fighting Right Beside Him," an
article by Regina Kahney, which appeared in *Gay Community News* and
The Body Politic. We appreciate their permission to use the material.

shirts!" she said. "And their mothers will scold them and spank them." It worked.) But it never occurred to her that Charlie was homosexual because, as she says, "I never thought that men were automatically macho. I thought men could be just as sensitive, just as tender, and love just as deeply as women."

As it turned out, Sarah was to know and care about two people her son loved very deeply. Although Charlie realized that he was gay at age thirteen, he did eventually marry and become the father of four children. He loved both his children and his wife, but the time came, after long internal searching, when he acknowledged to himself that he must meet his own needs, even though it meant leaving the family. And so John became the person with whom Charlie shared the remainder of his life.

Although Charlie had wanted to tell his mother about his gayness when he was eighteen and in the navy, he did not actually do so until he was thirty-five and about to move in with John. Sarah had been aware that "something was wrong" but did not know what had been troubling her son. Hiding her own initial shock and anguish, her response to the news was: "Charlie, you've been through an awful lot without me beside you, and since you're out in the open now, I'll never be a closet mother." (That last phrase, printed on a sign that Sarah Montgomery has since carried in Gay Pride parades, has become a legend.) At the time, she began to tell her relatives and friends about Charlie and found that because of her own matter-of-fact approach, most of them responded well. More to the point, she wrote her son asking him to *teach* her, to let her know what his gayness meant to him and to other gay people. And she urged her daughter-in-law to let the children know the truth about their father, not to hide it from them. This eventually happened, and the children were never denied access to him; indeed, as they grew up they spent many hours with their father and with John, whom they came to respect and to love dearly. Sarah says, "All the children, as it happens, have turned out nongay, which goes to disprove one more lie. Sexual orientation is not learned—it's just a fact of nature. Like myself, my grandchildren saw and knew closeup gay love." She insists, too: "Influence children? Nonsense! What is important is that young growing gay boys and lesbians have role models. It's terribly important that there be openly gay teachers in all the schools!"

Sarah spent quite a bit of time with Charlie and John in the next few years. At all times she was also welcomed into her grandchildren's home. She learned to love John as a son, and he to trust and care for her. She had no qualms about seeing them live together, and says, "I saw Charlie and John with a very beautiful, warm love. Love is love ... no matter how you slice it. ... I would be arrogant if I said I knew what it was like to be gay in a homophobic world. The best I could do was learn from my child and his lover, and take what I consider a deeply natural position."

Times changed for Charlie and John. They bought a house in the San Francisco suburbs to be near Charlie's children. Sarah visited them in late August 1972, only to learn in a devastating moment with her son that John had just been demoted by the company he'd been with for fifteen years. Charlie's own boss had also been questioning him since the purchase of the house. Sarah says, "Which way could they turn? Both of them had spent a whole lifetime in hiding, guilts, and suffering. Charlie's life—a double one while he was married—piled guilt upon guilt, rejection upon rejection. Charlie had always refused bigger jobs—for fear of exposure! Years and years of this. Oh, how I hate and fear the closet!"

During this entire visit both men shared their life stories, revealing much Sarah had never known about her son and the past years of John's life.

A short time later, back in New York, Sarah got word that on September 10 Charlie and John had locked themselves into their garage and turned on the car motor. She felt: "It was only [the threat of] job loss, nothing else in the world. There was no way to fight back. Two years ago they passed the gay rights bill in San Francisco, too late for my son and his lover."

Nine months after the death of her son, in June 1973, Sarah Montgomery, carrying her sign, "I Will *Not* Be a Closet Mother," marched with a host of others from Christopher Street to Central Park in the first Gay Pride Day parade in New York City. A few months later she heard of the newly formed Parents of Gays group, organized by Jeanne and Jules Manford; she joined up immediately and has become, as Jeanne puts it, "our star mentor." In the following year Sarah was the keynote speaker for the Gay Pride rally that followed the second annual parade. Speaking before a crowd of forty thousand gay people and their supporters, her simple but powerful words, coming from her heart, brought a cheer that may have been heard down at the Battery.

Sarah has counseled innumerable young people and scores of parents who are deeply troubled by the revelation that one of their children is gay. Remembering her own response to despair, she often says, "Ask your children to teach you. How else are you going to learn? What is meaningful to your child must be meaningful to you."

She has said, too, in recollection, "I read *The Well of Loneliness* when I was very young . . . [and] I remember one very wonderful remark. When [Stephen] told her father that she'd fallen in love with a woman, she said to him, 'How can it be wrong when it's the most beautiful thing that's ever happened to me in my life?' "

We are not all Sarah Montgomerys. Most of us are not faced with the ending of our child's life, and perhaps 'we could not face this situation with Sarah's fortitude if we were. But her story reveals a valuable lesson in the personal strength of a loving and learning attitude and the growth that at least one parent of a gay person has achieved.

At some point after our child has revealed her/his homosexuality, most of us realize that it's not going to go away. Any thought, vague or obsessive, that our child isn't *really* gay begins to disappear. And we discover that day-to-day life goes on, that within our families we must continue to deal with the reality of our child's gayness in whatever ways we can.

For many parents the response to their child's gayness has been *not* to deal with it at all, to pretend it doesn't exist, to live with the vain hope that some day Jill or Gary will meet the "right" man or woman. For others, hostility, anger, and their never-ceasing verbal campaign "against homosexuality" have created a serious rift between them and their child. There are plenty of discouraging stories. We knew fifteen-year-old Lee when he was kicked out of his house with nowhere to go. Young Jennie managed a brief phone call one day to tell us in despair of the new rules and restrictions that now confined her and isolated her from her friends and activities. And Nick, in his thirties, told us how his father had threatened him with a gun when he told him he was gay. Unfortunately, there are more tales of continuing tears, accusations, and threats—and sometimes the descent of total silence. But these stories represent a rather cheerless history, and they contribute little to our knowledge and ability to understand our own gay child.

It is more valuable to consider the ways families try to deal positively with the situation. *Do* most parents work it through? How do they come to accept and understand? What are the stumbling blocks? What are the "doors" to understanding?

The parents who find it easiest, of course, are those who, no matter what their inner feelings, realize right from the start that there is much they need to know and who are willing to listen to their child and to seek other ways to learn about homosexuality. This doesn't always happen all at once, even to the most open-minded of us; sometimes parents who believe themselves completely liberal on all subjects are surprised at their own reactions. Charlotte Spitzer, who has had wide experience as a marriage and family counselor and as a teacher of human sexuality in Los Angeles, tells us how it was for her.

I had known a few homosexuals along life's way, and I was not aware of feeling any prejudice against them. I was comfortable in their presence, and we got along well. In fact, when one of our good friends came to us and told us he was gay, we found that our relationship was strengthened rather than weakened.

Then, when my daughter Robin was about twenty-one, she told me she was gay. It hit me like the proverbial ton of bricks. I was devastated. How could I have brought such a thing on my child? Where had I gone wrong? I immediately assumed responsibility for her gayness.

I was quite surprised by my reactions; I would not have thought I would take it so hard. After all, I was an "enlightened woman." I even had a close friend who . . . I realized then that we can't predict how we will react to a given situation, even though we may think ourselves capable of handling it. How much harder it is to deal with information when it hits us emotionally than when we view it intellectually! So I hadn't really escaped my conditioning; I had merely covered it over. It was still deep within me, ready to surface when I got "hit" emotionally. . . .

When I could bring myself to look at the situation realistically, I decided to do everything in my power to get more information so as to better understand what homosexuality was all about. As I began to read, many of the myths with which I had grown up were dispelled. One day I attended a symposium on homosexuality, which helped enormously. In addition to getting much important information from authorities such as a gay minister and a psychologist who was researching the subject of homosexuality, I had an opportunity to hear a young gay woman speak. She reminded me very much of my daughter: beautiful, sensitive, creative, and bright. She spoke of her mother who avoided acceptance of her by persuading herself that this was only a phase her daughter was going through—at age twenty-five. The young woman expressed her sadness that she could not be closer to her mother, that this stood in the way of their relationship. She wanted to share herself and she could not. As I wept for the pain of the young speaker, I vowed that this would not happen to Robin and me.

It took a while to readjust my thinking, to gain perspective, and finally, to ask myself what I really wanted for my daughter. When I realized that I really wanted her to find happiness, love, and fulfillment in her own way, I found that I was "OK," and I felt that I had "arrived."

Charlotte now feels that her relationship with her daughter is better than ever, more open, honest, and loving, and that she is completely comfortable with her, her life-style, and her friends. She concludes that these friends are very much like her daughter, "sensitive, bright, and creative, and with a deep sense of commitment to each other."

Marguerite, a free-lance photographer and writer who lives in Minnesota, provides another story of "mixed feelings" and the process of working them through.

Larry told me he was gay under good circumstances, but I still took it as bad news.

I had just participated in a Sexual Attitudes Reassessment program in which homosexuality had been presented in exactly the same way as other sexual patterns, with films of committed couples. When I mentioned the program to my son, who was then seventeen, and spoke of the films of homosexual couples, he said that he thought he was like that, that he was bisexual, and preferred men.

I had a burst of conflicting thoughts and feelings. I was surprised, yet felt there must have been a reason why I had mentioned the films at that time. I was horrified, and yet I remembered the neutral way the subject was presented as just part of ordinary life. I felt that I had just told him that homosexuality was OK, but that really didn't mean it was OK for *him*.

Larry was speaking quietly, with what appeared to be flashes of apprehension and determination. I'm sure I showed surprise and some shock. I felt I hadn't a leg to stand on, for I had started the conversation in a reasonable, conversational manner, and he was replying in the same way. Now, suddenly, the topic had become frightening and I had to struggle to remain reasonable.

When I asked him if he was "sure," he said that he was, that he had a lover who was a wonderful person, that they were close and loved each other. I was glad he had that closeness because I thought he had been lonely sometimes as a teenager, but I was sorry that it was with a man. I suspected that he had been taken advantage of by an older man we both knew. (About six years older, and a dancer! Is it true what they say about dancers? I wondered.) I think I told him I believed homosexuality was OK in general, but I was having a hard time accepting it for him. I felt I was turning myself inside out to be reasonable and understanding.

It helped to meet my son's "friend." (Larry used the term *lover,* but I didn't like to.) He seemed like a very nice young man. Again, a mixed reaction. I was surprised, but also *not* surprised—of course Larry would pick someone nice like himself.

About six months later I told two good women friends about Larry. Their reaction was reassuring. They both knew and liked Larry and thought there could be much worse news. After all, he was still alive and healthy, not a criminal or hooked on drugs. They thought it was a serious issue but did not turn away from me in any way. . . .

Two other things had an impact on me. One was a visit to a counselor at the university. This man didn't directly answer my questions about causes and dangers. Instead he helped me clarify what I wanted for myself in my relationship with Larry: continuing contact, reassurance that we could have a mother-son relationship that I could enjoy and that wouldn't hurt him or drive him away. I also did a *Gestalt* exercise in which I was first myself and then Larry. When I took Larry's position (to "be" him), I felt a wave of loneliness at not being understood or accepted.

The other helpful event at the time was finding an article by the mother of a lesbian in *Family Circle* at my local grocery store. What a respectable source! The story of the mother's initial negative reaction and her changing response made me hopeful. She described her daughter's lesbian friends in positive terms and said she could enjoy their visits to her home. That gave me a glimpse of a possible good future to replace the wonderful imagined one I had built up in my head while Larry was growing up, and which had been lost with his announcement.

Kay and Lloyd C., who live outside Milwaukee, are a couple whose religious beliefs guide and strengthen every aspect of their lives. When they learned, in 1974, that their son Jon was gay, it seemed to them a terrible and unbelievable revelation. Yet only two years later they accepted an invitation to participate in a panel discussion of homosexuality at the Chicago Circle Center of Illinois University. Part of Kay's presentation follows:

This is the first time I have spoken publicly about our son's homosexuality. Even though the anticipation of talking to an audience unknown to us has caused some anxiety, still, when such an opportunity comes, I must try to do whatever I can to ease the problems that confront homosexuals dealing with whether to tell or not to tell their parents, and also to ease the problems that confront parents when told about their son's or daughter's preference.

So much unnecessary unhappiness is caused by attitudes on the part of parents who are unyielding, unapproachable, unkind, hostile. I can understand the confusion, the pain, and the shock which surround a son's or daughter's revelation that they are gay. It happened to us, too. We are not a unique couple; we traveled the same route that most parents do—victims of an unaccepting society, maybe more accurately a part of this very society which through the centuries has caused so much damage to homosexuals by both spoken and implied attitudes; these attitudes have permeated the churches as well.

Our first reaction came in the form of questions: Is Jon sick? Is he unstable, perverted? Is it shameful? Can we pray and have hope that God will change him? Is it our fault?

But the great thing is that we learned, we grew, and we began to understand. We came to know that being gay can be right. We read that homosexuality exists all over the world and has always existed. We came to know that it is not an evil or a disgusting affliction. It is not an emotional disease, or a grave moral sin that separates an unrepentant homosexual from the love and grace of God. We began to realize that homosexuality is part of the range of normal human behavior, that being gay is not a choice—it cannot be given up or reversed or counseled away, or lost by meeting the right girl!

How did we come to these conclusions? First of all, my husband and I had many long, enlightening talks with Jon. At times we cried together, hugged each other. All the time Jon knew that our love for him remained steadfast, maybe even grew deeper for him as we became aware of his inner struggles to accept himself as he was. Then we also read many articles and pamphlets and books—some good, some not. We talked with many of Jon's gay friends, most of them men and women of Chicago's Metropolitan Community Church.

The very hardest part of all this for us [came early], when we saw Jon telling God to get out of his life, blaming God for this "hell" in which he lived, a hell created by society, not God.

The most wonderful and rewarding time was coming to Chicago to the Metropolitan Community Church and worshiping with Jon, knowing that God was number one in his life once more. We sensed that his faith and trust in God had grown and deepened in his search for the truth. Our faith and trust had grown deeper also. He accepted himself as a homosexual and was assured that God did too.

In a subsequent letter to his parents, Jon paid tribute to their successful efforts to learn and understand:

Today I just stopped to realize how very fortunate I am to have parents like you. I feel that I can be totally myself around both of you; my lover feels that way too. No words could ever thank you enough.

Sometimes, the "revelation" comes as an accidental discovery, as with Faith and Ed. Faith relates these events:

The Parents' Story

In the fall of 1969, our son, Deke, then twenty-five, was living with us and working in Phoenix prior to a move to San Francisco in January. Through us, at a party the previous summer, he had met an older sophisticated European professor and artist who we knew was gay. During the fall I began to wonder why he and Ted were corresponding, and by Christmas I was very troubled when Deke announced that he had accepted Ted's offer of renting a room in his apartment in San Francisco. Perhaps had I told Deke why I was upset that he would be living with Ted, the truth would have come out in a much less unfortunate way, for in retrospect I'm sure he would have told us then and there that it was OK—he was gay, too.

As matters turned out, two letters arrived in the mail one day in January (before Deke left for San Francisco)—one to Deke and one a Christmas note to us—in identical envelopes. Inadvertently, without looking carefully, I opened Deke's instead of ours, and to my utter dismay saw that it was a love letter from Ted. It was a total shock, although I realize now that I had been pushing away suspicions for some time, always making myself believe he couldn't be gay because he had always had girl friends.

We talked it over that evening. I said all the wrong things, and Ed expressed his dismay. We were never angry at Deke, but afraid that Ted would "corrupt" our son. I recall saying, "I'd rather die than have you live with him," which naturally upset him greatly. Ed was wonderfully calm and wanted to know why he hadn't told us before. Deke replied that he was afraid it would upset us too much. He was greatly relieved to have it out at last.

There was never any hostility at any time. It turned out that his three sisters had known for some time and it had in no way affected their deep love for and appreciation of him. They were most helpful in making us realize that this was not unusual and that it was not my fault or Ed's. When he departed for San Francisco a few weeks later, he knew we were on the way to understanding how he felt, what he was, and that our love and respect for him was just as profound.

Since then, during many visits home, we have had many long talks with him, opening the years from his first sexual stirrings at around ten, his having no one he felt he could talk with and get answers from. He told us that the eight years from age twelve to his first gay relationship at college were the most miserable of his life. We never suspected that there was anything unusual bothering him outside of normal teenage frustrations, for he was basically such a cheerful, easy-to-live-with, creative, affectionate person and was always crazy about some girl all through his high school years. He is still bisexual but feels more comfortable with, and attracted to, his own sex.

We are continually indebted to Deke for his patience and understanding, and for opening our minds to what being gay means, and for the many helpful books he has given us. Both Ed and I feel comfortable enough now to be able to talk about our son's gayness with pride.

As we see, parents can and do come to understand and accept their homosexual children. The process happens over varying periods of time, and it might be helpful to examine in greater detail just how that process of change takes place. Jim and Mona, who live in Missouri, recorded their experience for us. This couple learned for certain that their son, Rick, was gay when they were visiting him in San Francisco during Christmas vacation of 1973. Their older daughter, Laura, lived near him there, and their youngest child, Suzi, had come west with her parents. Rick, twenty-two at the time, was working on his master's degree in clinical psychology; since then he has completed his doctorate. Here, Mona and Jim recollect their experiences and feelings at the time and bring them up to the present.

MONA: We were all sitting around in Laura's apartment in San Francisco one evening, and Rick finally said he had something to tell us. He hemmed and hawed for about five minutes, saying that he was nervous, that he didn't know how to approach this, that it might be upsetting to us, and so on.... Now, from the age of fifteen or sixteen, when other boys in his class were dating, Rick did not date, although he did have many opportunities, and he had women friends as well as male friends.

At any rate, Jim and I suspected that he might be gay (although he later told us he had no gay relationships until he was about twenty). Certainly, since he was not dating, the idea had crossed our minds many times.

So, when he told us, it was not a great shock to me. The way he put it was that he "had love for other men." That was the phrase he used.

My reaction was sort of a nonreaction, and I just felt, well, this is it. Now it's confirmed, what we suspected or feared. I felt it was very important to express confidence in him, and I said something like, "All right, it's not a big deal. We care for you just the same, and nothing is different."

JIM: I recall that incident a little differently. It's true that we both had the suspicion because of his not dating girls during high school and afterward, but I had hoped that this was temporary, that he would grow out of it. (I had been sort of slow dating myself.) Besides, we had talked to a psychologist who was a friend of the family, who had worked with Rick, and he told us that he had seen no evidence that Rick was homosexual. So while in one sense it wasn't a terrible surprise, it was also a real blow to me.

As I recall it, the scene got pretty emotional. Rick started to sob, and I acted on the impulse to go over and put my arms around him and just hold him, and just not say anything, just to let him know I was present to him and that no matter what he had done in his life, he was important to me—something like that. We were helped in this situation in that Rick was very close to Laura, who is a year and a half older. She had known about Rick's gayness and, in the San Francisco climate in which they were living, and in the generation that they were a part of, this was not as traumatic as it was to me; and Laura sort of helped give perspective. She had a number of friends, both men and women, who were gay.

Our younger daughter, Suzi, was with us at the time, and I feel good, in retrospect, that Rick was willing to share the fact of his gayness with all of us in the family.

We had a couple of positive things going for us. One is that we had all been in group communication experiences, group therapy, at different times, not necessarily together. Out of that we had learned to use communication skills in the family. And since we only got together c :asionally, we would say, "OK, let's have a family session," where we would get our feelings and wants out. The second thing was that since Rick was in this degree program, he was under the supervision of a therapist, and this therapist had offered to meet with Rick and all of us if we wanted to. So the next day we went down to his office and had a session—for about an hour and a half. There, under this man's direction, we had a chance to really get in touch with the variety of feelings we had, and I think that was really important in helping *me,* anyway, get around an important corner on the situation.

MONA: Despite all this, we had a wonderful time in San Francisco. This particular event brought us closer, and since the whole family was there together, there was not going to be the problem of telling other children in the family.

I guess you could say I have accepted it completely, intellectually. But part of me still finds it difficult—I have some guilt that this indicates some error on my part or some weakness on Rick's part. This feeling is sort of irrational or emotional, but outwardly, at least, we talk about it when we get together. We joke about it, too. Rick feels free to tell us about his relationships; he talks about his lovers; and we feel free to ask questions—not intimate questions, but we are pretty open.

Occasionally I feel pangs of regret and guilt, and two or three times I have cried over it a long time, but as time goes on, I think I can accept it emotionally as well. I think I do have some feelings about "what the neighbors would think"—that sort of thing. Jim and I have no living parents, so we don't have to worry about what they would think. If they were alive, they would probably have a lot of difficulty accepting this.

JIM: I must say, I had mixed feelings from the beginning. When Rick first told me, I felt a strong impulse to give him personal support. But within a very short time I found I had a lot of worried and negative feelings. I had grown up with all the stereotypes about homosexuals, and Rick did have a few effeminate mannerisms. I really wanted very much to hope that this was a temporary thing. I hoped that because he was under the supervision of a therapist at the time, he could work his way back to heterosexuality. I realize now that's an illusion, that he's not going to change, and I have to accept that.

When he was younger we seemed to have trouble hitting it off. I have always been very athletic. Rick was slender, small-boned. He didn't pick up my interest in sports. I made a deliberate effort not to lay that on him, to try to move where he was, but as he was growing up, I felt bad many times that I didn't know how to relate to him better. . . .

About a year after he told us I signed up for a sex education class, and one time some homosexuals came in for a two-and-a-half-hour session. In listening and talking to them, I found how severe the kinds of discrimination were, the negative attitudes that they experienced, and I really became angry that a group of human beings in our society, who are not really doing anything hurtful to anyone, against anyone's will, would have to suffer pain and handicaps of that order.

Gradually Mona and I decided that we wanted to try to be of some help, although we have moved very slowly. But I have tried to find occasions where I could meet homosexual men and women as *people*—and that has made a big difference in my attitude toward the situation in general.

MONA: I think that what has helped me most has been telling a few people about Rick and finding acceptance; also visiting the Metropolitan Community Church. Maybe the most helpful thing was discussing it in a Transactional Analysis group I was in for about a year. The group was very supportive and accepting, and I worked through some things there having to do with Rick in a way that was extremely helpful.

I have two older sisters and an older brother and I have told them. They are all supportive and I think it has brought us slightly closer. . . .

JIM: I, too, have told my sister who lives here in the same town. We have always had a good relationship, and we have shared certain bad times of each of our kids. She did not treat this news as something extraordinary, so I'm glad I shared that with her. We also have told the minister in our church that we are available if parents or anybody wants to talk with us. [But] nothing has really happened. . . . Another thing I have done is to write letters whenever I've taken exception to the stereotyping of gays on TV programs. That's about where we are in terms of involvement, which, let's face it, is minimal.

MONA: [Because] our son lives far away from us, we have not been closely involved in the day-to-day problems of his life, although he tells us about them in his letters and tapes. As it is, I would say that knowing that Rick is gay has not changed our lives in any big way. Some negative aspects, I suppose, are trying to cope with guilt and hurt, and trying to figure out what we ought to be doing for the cause, but not doing much. On the other hand, I think that we still have a very good relationship with our son and our other children, maybe a better one than we might have had otherwise. We have worked at trying to be open with each other and at encouraging Rick to be open with us, which he is. I have worked at letting the issue of homosexuality come out repeatedly, and we deal with feelings on both sides, so it has not been a problem among us.

JIM: I continue to have mixed feelings. I have moved a long way toward an accepting attitude, but when I am candid, I will admit that if I could choose it, I wouldn't have chosen it this way. I regret the idea that we won't have grandchildren with my name, but I agree with Mona that we have had to get our real basic values straightened out by facing this. Rick is my son, the same person who was the infant and the child, the boy and the adolescent in my life and my affection for him comes first. I have a lot of pride in his academic and career accomplishments. He got a Ph.D. at a very early age. He has a responsible job as a clinical psychologist in a hospital. He has pioneered in a gay clinic for parents of gays. So he's making a useful contribution in the world for people who experience a lot of pain, and I'm very proud of that.... Each time we talk and I get a sense of his life unfolding, I am forced to do some more growing. I can see him more as the person he *is*. Also, I am learning to see a whole group of people differently. I always looked at gay people through a pair of distorted glasses, seeing them in terms of the ho-ho-ho jokes and ideas that I experienced in the culture. I am learning to see them as human beings, as persons to whom I can relate in ways that are good for me—thereby giving up a set of habits that caused me to ignore, or distort my views on, gay people in the community. I feel that I can become a healthier human being by accepting this group of people that I was always taught to reject.

Jim and Mona each indicated that their initial expressed feelings of support and love for their son were later supplanted by an awareness of pain and negative feelings. How often we have heard parents say, "I feel as if I'm taking one step forward and two backward."

One young woman once told us how supportive her mother was in her first letter after she knew. The tone of this comment allowed us to say, "And then you got the *second* letter!" She said, "How did you know? Yes, her second letter was hurt and angry. I don't understand it." This is a natural part in any change. When we view these "backward steps"—the surfacing of long-held beliefs and prejudices—in the perspective of a process, they need not be too distressing. Change, particularly in an area as deeply seated and hidden as human sexuality has been in American culture, *is* a slow process. But with attitudes as open, and efforts as deliberate, as those displayed by Mona and Jim and their children, change can and will occur.

Sarah Gaylord experienced a painful degree of "aftershock," one that brought months of anguish to both her and her daughter Wendy. Excerpts from their detailed stories follow; Sarah speaks first:

Wendy was a child of the sixties. In 1974 she was enrolled as a freshman at Kent State University. One day, as we stood together in the kitchen, my mind circulating around a grocery list, Wendy looked radiant and, in her inimitable throaty voice, said, "Mom, I have something to tell you when you return from the store."

My curiosity piqued, I responded, "Come on, that's not fair. Tell me now." She resisted momentarily, giggled, blushed, and then out came those words: "I'm gay."

I felt absolutely nothing. She could just as simply have been saying that the sun rises each morning. Her words had no impact upon me. . . . I was completely unruffled, undented. I suffered no mental rape, no emotional breakdown . . . at least not then. Not until I was pushing a shopping cart through the supermarket did I begin to feel a slight twinge in my belly, and not until that evening did those words, "I'm gay," crush me utterly. I felt I'd been run over by a boulder rumbling down Mt. Kilimanjaro.

I had visions of Wendy being taunted, ostracized, and stoned by monstrous crowds . . . of Wendy in sexual encounters with other women, and I made myself feel nauseated. Sometimes it was hard to separate myself from those "monstrous crowds" because I, too, condemned her sexuality as sick, abnormal, vile —and the sensation was all-consuming and powerfully destructive.

Gut-racking sobs choked me each night before exhaustion overtook me, and weeping filled my days wherever I was, whatever I was doing. . . . "Wendy, my beautiful baby girl . . . WHY?" echoed through me for months. . . .

Nor was there any relief when I tried to "talk sense" to Wendy or force her to withdraw herself from Kent Gay Liberation Front and from "all those people who were brainwashing her."

The wall went up between us just when she needed my understanding, acceptance, and support for what she had been through during her years of teenage confusion and turmoil. I failed to reward the tremendous courage she had demonstrated in trusting me, her mother, by confiding in me. I failed to be sensitive to the overwhelming relief she felt in "coming out."

Much later, after months of unhappiness and dissension between my daughter and me, I asked myself the most meaningful and soul-searching questions: What right do I have to force my fears and needs and dreams upon another human being, especially upon that life which I carried *in trust* in my womb eighteen years ago? What right do I have to play around with the emotions of someone I profess to love unconditionally? Ultimately the only humane and loving answer came to me loud and clear: NONE. . . .

I now feel certain Wendy will reach her fullest potential, that is, to be loved and loving in her intimate relationships.

Wendy recalls it all this way:

My mother's immediate reaction to the news was no reaction. She said, "We'll talk about it later." We didn't talk about it later; we *yelled* about it later. Armed with only that piece of information ("I am gay"), she started firing such accusations at me as "You hate men." "You hate life." "Lesbians kill each other when they break up."

None of this was true but I didn't know how to protect myself. My education had never taught me to defend my homosexuality. There were no open homosexuals to talk with in high school. As a matter of fact, the isolation and lack of truthful education on the subject had led me to the conclusion that I was the only lesbian in Ohio! The only education I had received on the matter was being expressed by my mother.

The tension between us after that surpassed even the tension I had lived with while "in the closet." Never before had my mother withdrawn herself from me. She wouldn't even hold eye contact with me, much less a civilized conversation. For I had violated the traditions with which she had been raised and with which she thought she had raised me.

With each tension-filled month that passed I came closer and closer to resigning myself to the fact that I had lost my mother. Were it not for the advice of my gay friends, who had experienced the trials and tribulations of telling their parents, I probably would have given up on my mother, given up on the hopes that someday she would accept my lesbianism, that someday I would be free to bring home my girl friends as my brothers did.

I stuck it out, not without depression. I ignored her when she said I was turning into a man because I wore bib overalls.

Finally, in May of 1975, I decided that the tension must end. I wanted my mother back. I sent her a long letter and some literature. When I received a reply I felt as though I had a new mother. During the time between our last conversation and my letter, she had met a lesbian and had finally learned some truths about homosexuality. Her response revealed this: "If I can't accept your homosexuality as an individual human difference, then that's like my not being able to accept the fact that your favorite color is yellow and mine is orange."

As we have seen earlier, growing up gay is seldom easy, and for some young people it's harder than for others. Lee has three children: a daughter and a son, both now married with children, and Steve, the youngest, now twenty-five. When he was about eleven, Steve began to skip school, run away from home, and even to steal. On the advice of a juvenile counselor, he was placed in a foster home for a while. When he returned, he became very destructive and once threatened to kill his father. Lee later learned that although he had hidden it at the time, Steve had had homosexual relationships with his cousin and also with his own father, who had initiated them. It became clear then to Lee why Steve hated his father so much. There were seemingly constant arguments and tension (Lee and her husband had not been getting along well for years anyway), and now Steve's father was constantly berating all three children, especially Steve. Finally, after a big argument when Steve threatened his father, the judge in juvenile court ordered Steve to a thirty-day observation period in a mental hospital. Although the doctors noted that he was going through a difficult adjustment from boyhood to young manhood, they said nothing about his being homosexual. Meanwhile, Lee and her husband agreed to divorce, and after both older children had left home, she and Steve went to live in New York City. This was in 1967.

The remainder of Lee's story is in her own words, taken from a taped interview she made in San Diego in July 1977.

We went to New York to live with my parents, but due to circumstances that had nothing to do with Steve, I found I couldn't live with them, so we moved to a hotel. Well, Steve, who was then fifteen, spent his evenings out on his own; he said he went to the YMCA, to movies, and so on. He was always in by ten-thirty—the curfew time in New York at that time. One night he didn't come home at the usual time. I was very concerned, and at two o'clock in the morning I received a telephone call from the police department; they said they had my son in custody, and that he was picked up standing on the corner of Forty-second Street and Times Square—out after curfew. So I went to the police station and got him. They told me nothing except that we had to report to juvenile court the next morning.

We went down to the court and Steve was taken into one room and I into another, with a policewoman. She said, "Do you know why your son was picked up?" I said, "No... the curfew hours?" And she said, "No, he was picked up and booked as being a teenage male hooker."

Well, I was shocked. "You must be wrong, not Steve... a hooker? Women are hookers, not men." And she said, "Well, my dear, I don't know how much you know—but..." And then she proceeded to tell me about the homosexuals. Well, I had never really discussed homosexuality, because I never had any reason to. And I said, "I don't believe you, it's a lie. Steve— *no*, no way—no way, Steve is *not!*" And I was crying, hysterical. She said, "I'll bring your son in, and he can tell you." Steve came in and I said, "Steve, is it true?" "Mom, I've been wanting to tell you for a long time, but I knew how hurt you'd be and I just couldn't do it."

Jeff, who told us about growing up gay in Chapter 2, is another young man who struggled desperately with himself in younger years. His mother and he share more of their story with us. Lucille Moses recalls the early years:

I had never thought or had reason to think of his being gay. He was at one time engaged to a lovely girl and said he was going to marry her, and I was delighted. Then she became pregnant, and I could see that he was having many problems. After his father died, I had much trouble with him; he seemed to resent, and actually dislike, me. One day he left me a note and said not to worry, that he was going to be gone for a week and would be all right. I started to worry when he did not return after a week. I finally called his college. They found him and suggested he see a psychiatrist. Then the trouble really began. He started to move his things out of the house and was very cold and rude to me. There was a long time when I didn't see him or have any contact with him at all. He was living on campus and was to graduate in the spring. The Vietnam war was on, and we had often talked about how horrible it was.

Then he wrote again that he was going away, and I realized he was on the verge of a nervous breakdown. I was frantic, and finally I did get some information about him, but I was told that he could not deal with either the girl he was to marry or me. I was told to keep my distance and that he was not going to get in touch with me. Long after, he told me that at that time he was very close to ending his life. He did get drawn into the war, and because he had a close escape from death on three different occasions, he reviewed everything in a different light. So he wrote to me and asked me to forgive him. I remember weeping and weeping over that beautiful letter. I wrote him that I had never stopped loving him and there was nothing to forgive.

All this might have given me a clue to his latent homosexuality; I don't know. The only time I was puzzled was when I came across a book in his room with pictures of men in very tight clothing. I did wonder then, but only in a vague way.

I knew for certain, however, when he came to visit me with this fellow. I don't think it would have occurred to me to *ask* Jeff about being homosexual if it weren't that the other fellow was so devoid of personality, so completely shallow, that I couldn't imagine what Jeff would have in common with him. I realize now that I would have had the same feeling if Jeff had chosen a woman who, outwardly, wouldn't have much to contribute to a relationship. I may have done this fellow a grave injustice, because I am sure he was self-conscious and felt intimidated by the situation.

So—as Jeff has reminded me—I posed the question to him. We talked, I remember, behind closed doors for at least two hours. . . . All the things I had read or heard about homosexuals and their relationships—all of the propaganda—suddenly flooded my mind, and I felt literally sick. At that time I don't think I realized that homosexuals could have *good* relationships, based on qualities other than physical attraction.

Of course, I didn't act like an outraged parent—I couldn't. I have always loved my son. I was just sick in spirit and felt his life was ruined. He had literally been snatched from death in Vietnam and now, here was this. I guess I must have told him that if it had been someone more his equal (that word now sounds very harsh and wrong) in intelligence, talent, philosophy—whatever—I could bear it better.

I didn't love my son any less, but I kept his homosexuality in my *own* private closet. When he finally met someone whom I could respect, I felt relieved and much better—but as I told both of them, they had my tolerance, but not my understanding.

As Lucille has told us in Chapter 2, Jeff's subsequent letter about his young life brought her total understanding, and the cycle of change was complete.

We have found over the years, and in gathering material for this book, that each individual experience is of human interest in itself and is also valuable in understanding ourselves and others better. Here are the stories of four mothers who have worked through their own feelings in different ways and to different levels of acceptance:

Margaret is in her sixties, the product of a fairly protected upbringing. She is a dedicated and loving woman who was deeply shocked by her son's revelation. And yet, over a period of some two years, Margaret came to understand and support not only her son but also the cause of gay people. About a year after she found out she told us this story:

I am a widow and the mother of three adult children who have been on their own for many years. My eldest son, who lives across the country from me, has master's degrees in business and engineering. My daughter lives in the South, and she has several advanced educational credentials also. My youngest son, Bob, earned his Ph.D. in literature and is an accomplished musician. He now lives near me, after teaching in another state for three years.

It seemed that he came back here at the time I needed him most, as my mother was failing in health and she loved Bob. His visits with her meant so much to her, and he had such concern for her. He has always been so considerate of her and me, never failing to remember birthdays and special occasions (when my other children forgot), and he is so thoughtful in many ways. I have always felt very close to him because of this. When my husband died suddenly in the early sixties, Bob was the most comfort to me of all the children.

One summer evening in 1974, Bob told me he was a homosexual. I just couldn't believe it. He is so intelligent and artistic and has such high ideals, I was stunned. My idea of a homosexual was someone you wouldn't want to associate with because of all the trash you read in the paper. It broke my heart to think that he had been carrying this burden alone for so many years because he was afraid to tell his family. In so many cases the family disowns them when they find out about their son or daughter.

Of course, I cried every night for a week, and prayed to God, "Why him?" Bob had always been a wonderful son, never giving me any trouble and doing only good to others. When he was studying for his Ph.D. and teaching and had a church job, too, he always found time to listen to any of his students or friends who had problems.

I finally made an appointment with my doctor, as I needed someone to talk to and I thought there was no one in the family available. He helped me very much . . . told me I should be thankful Bob had not been born with any serious physical problems. Afterward, I talked with my daughter, and she was very understanding, as Bob had already told her without my knowledge.

This has never lessened my love for Robert. In fact, I love him more because I know he needs me and my understanding and backing.

I have met a number of Bob's gay friends, and have attended the Metropolitan Community Church a few times; everyone seems unusually friendly, and shows concern for the other person. If most gay people are like these, we need them to make a better world tomorrow.

Nina lives in Virginia, and when we first heard from her some years ago she was beginning to deal very well with her daughter's being gay. At the time she first wrote, she had decided she might work with other parents, but as it turned out, her efforts to reach others were unsuccessful, and she became discouraged. This is her story of the "revelation" and what happened thereafter.

Doris confronted me in person (when I went to visit her in July 1974 and to attend our church conference) with the fact that she considered herself a lesbian, that she and her lover were soon going to move in together, that she was involved in gay activist groups, that she had come out to all her friends, that she had never been happier in her life. I was absolutely devastated! How could it be? What had I done wrong? My first reaction was to take the next plane home and perhaps never see her again. How could we possibly relate to each other now? She might as well be dead. We had always been so close. Why, why, why?

She persuaded me to stay that night at least. She talked and talked, and I cried and cried. She gave me books and I read all night. The next morning she went to work and I roamed the streets, but I could find no answers. That night we talked more, and I tried to tell her I loved her but that I had to have time to think.

The conference started the next day, and Doris urged me to go to the gay workshop, although she herself was not going to be there. I did, with fear and trembling. But that meeting was the best thing that ever happened. I listened to the conversation of those present, the little exercises they were led in by Millie, an attractive young woman. The things they were saying and doing were all strange to me, but they seemed like such kind, thoughtful, sincere people—somewhat troubled by their life-style, but mostly because of others. They seemed happy enough. I hadn't been able to believe Doris when she had said that she was happy.

I finally told them why I was there, and they all talked about their parents and the hurts they had caused and suffered, the sadness of having parents unable to accept and understand them. They gave me encouragement and advice. From then on I began to be able to think somewhat rationally . . . and to talk with Doris. . . . She did want me to meet Karen and get to know her, but I couldn't. . . . But I went home feeling that, gay or straight, I had a wonderful daughter.

One year later I was able to suggest that she and Karen meet

me in Harrisburg and we'd all drive to that summer's conference together and thus get to know each other. It turned out to
be a beautiful idea. Karen was nervous and so was I—but I
found that to know Karen was to love her. Later, I was disappointed that Karen couldn't come home with Doris for the
holidays. I didn't think it could ever be this way.

Nina relates that some time later Doris came home and
spoke as a lesbian at their local church. It was, as Nina puts
it, her, Nina's, coming out. But she says that since her
daughter spoke before their congregation, "no one ever
mentions her to me. None of my friends who know her and
about her work with the Gay Caucus ever ask about her. I
occasionally try to bring her into the conversation when they
are bragging about their children and grandchildren—I'm
proud of her, too!—but there's no follow-up. I feel that
everyone avoids talking about her."

And she still acknowledges that "being the parent of a
gay is not a totally comfortable thing," but perhaps when
she does reach the point of being "totally comfortable" with
her daughter's sexual orientation, her friends will sense that
and, taking the cue from Nina, will be more open to talking
about Doris.

Lisa learned many years ago that her son was gay, long
before there was anything available in the way of support
or general information for parents. Like so many parents
in the past, she had to work it through pretty much by
herself.

When my son, now thirty, was in the eleventh grade, he told
me he thought he was gay. I was a widow at the time, and both
of us went through a stage of confusion and great upset. We
lived in Columbus, Ohio—a very conservative environment in
school, society, etc.—so he was quite unhappy. We both decided he should see a psychiatrist, which he did for several
months. It did not do much for him, except allow him to talk
to someone besides me.

I am a very liberal person and my son and I (and my husband when he was alive) shared a very close relationship with each other. At my son's request, he went to the twelfth grade in the East, to get out of Columbus. There he got some better counseling. I know, too, that my full acceptance of him and understanding and never-ending love made his adjustment a lot easier.

During the following years he lived at home part of the time, some in the East, and then in San Francisco where it is so much easier for gay people. I visit him a lot, and he comes home for long visits, feeling good about himself, and he is always welcome to bring friends and lovers to my house.

Through the years, I exposed myself to the gay scene, going to gay bars with him and befriending his gay friends, and often counseling them. I have never had any trouble communicating with them, and they always say, I wish my parents felt the way you do.

Barry wrote a beautiful letter to his parents, Peg and Bill, telling of his bisexual orientation, while he was a student at Stanford University in 1969. Peg, who with her husband lives in New England, tells of their reactions from the point of view of seven years later.

I know we were much more upset than we ever let on to Barry. For that reason, it was just as well that he was so far away. And though we did call him on the phone to reassure him, we did not let him see the full range of our reactions because we did not want him to feel sorry he had shared with us. . . . And I am sure he would have been distressed if he could have seen how teary I was for a good while. I did react just as he feared I would, that somehow I was "to blame." I had to do a lot of reading and learning to rid myself of that particular notion. . . .

We were not well informed either about homosexuality or about life as gays experience it, so it was a great help to us that we had our friend and Barry's, our minister, to talk to. He was very matter-of-fact and unemotional about it; also he recommended that we get together our whole family and have some sessions with an analyst friend who did family therapy (and was himself bisexual) to explore what this new information meant to all of us. We didn't have time for many of these sessions (for various family reasons). But, anyhow, we started down the road of learning and at the same time of realizing in retrospect how foolish we had been not to realize all along about Barry's sexuality. We had a strong desire *not* to see what was right there staring us in the face; there's no doubt about that.

To this day I would have to say that I think his chances of happiness would be greater if he were heterosexual, but that's because there is so much dislike and discrimination in our society.

Most of the parents we have heard from or about have moved beyond their initial heartaches, fears, and doubts; they have come to see a new aspect of their gay child's life in a fresh and realistic perspective. All of us can learn from each other, and we do, as we share our experiences and relate how we eliminated our old beliefs and attitudes. The process of change, as many of us have said again and again, is one that has enriched our lives and enhanced our awareness of ourselves, of our children, and of other people.

4

What Is Gay?

This is a pretty presumptuous chapter title. We can no more tell you all about gay people in these pages than we could about straight people in the same space. Would you expect to find yourself precisely described in a chapter on "The Heterosexual Man and Woman"? Unlikely. But we can give you an idea of some feelings that gay people have about themselves and each other, and some idea of what it's like to be gay. One thing we're not going to be able to tell you is what all gay Americans are like. Nobody can describe twenty million people in one chapter. And in our discussion of gays and gay life-styles we speak only from our experience as parents and friends of gay people, not as professional psychiatrists. Not that professional psychiatrists themselves are all experts. As one famous psychiatrist reportedly said to another, "All my homosexual patients are sick." To which the other is said to have replied, "So are all my heterosexual patients."

Until late in the 1960s, no one had ever made objective studies of mentally healthy, self-accepting gay people; it was widely assumed that they did not exist. This was partly because the vast majority of gay women and men do not openly reveal their sexual preference. Homosexual mental patients (many of whom hoped to be "cured") and the minority of gays who act out an obtrusively macho "dyke" or swishy "faggot" manner seemed to many people to represent the norm. As a result, particularly in this country, homosexuality was for many years widely considered to be a form of mental illness.

Today, as we know, that situation has improved considerably. Both the American Psychiatric and American Psychological societies have officially declared that gays as a group are not sick, and increased media coverage of the subject has been quite helpful. Furthermore, gay people from all walks of life have begun to come out of the closet, choosing to affirm their identity instead of denying it. There are many excellent books and articles by and about healthy, well-adjusted gays, although this literature is not as widely known as we might wish.

We want to emphasize that we have known hundreds of gay people and loved many of them. We have seen for ourselves that being homosexually oriented doesn't make one sick, or immoral, or criminally inclined. A lifetime of persecution and self-denial can produce such people quite effectively in some cases, but there is no inherent predisposition in homosexuals toward emotional instability or antisocial behavior. More and more gay people, especially the younger ones, are realizing that there is no reason to feel guilty about their sexual orientation. They know that they can best achieve a rewarding, socially productive life, not by denying that identity, but by affirming it.

In this book we have limited our definition of *gay* to men and women who are predominantly *homosexual*, meaning that their strongest emotional and sexual responses are aroused by individuals of the same rather than of the opposite sex. Their gender identity is normal—that is to say, the men think of themselves as men and the women value their own womanliness. Few hate or mistrust members of the opposite sex; they just don't feel sexually attracted to them. Emotionally healthy, self-accepting gay people are likely to form warm friendships with persons of both sexes, irrespective of sexual orientation.

Aside from the self-identified gay people who form the subject of this book, there is another category of persons who are attracted by members of their own biological gender: *transsexuals*, who think of themselves as being members of the opposite sex. A certain number of them, such as Renee Richards, have had the time and money to undergo the difficult surgical process of a sex-change operation. This is still relatively rare. Most transsexuals suffer some degree of persistent disorientation, since they are forced to assume an identity and a social role that seem unnatural to them. They are not physically attracted by persons who seem to be the same sex as themselves, but by people whom they perceive to be totally different.

Bud is a biologically male transsexual, a well-groomed, affable executive secretary of fifty who thinks of himself as "a woman trapped in a man's body." Bud despises gay men and does not care to associate too closely with them. Most of his good friends are women or married couples. His sexual preference runs to "straight," generally married men of aggressively masculine manner and appearance; he is a great admirer of dark, abundant body hair. Policemen and sailors, located through friends or by cruising known pickup areas, have been his most satisfying contacts in the past. He enjoys playing the role of "another woman" in the lives of his lovers, and knows that he can provide a variety of sexual experience that is intensely pleasurable to many comfortably heterosexual men. Bud would have undergone a surgical sex change years ago if that had been available on a routine basis. But given his limited income, with the expenses of his suburban home to maintain, and the difficulty of making a new life at his age, this is only a dream.

Many people also confuse homosexuals with *transvestites* —men and women who cross-dress. Transvestite men enjoy wearing women's clothes, commonly in private or at gay social functions. The majority are primarily or exclusively "straight"; that is, their sexual preference runs to women. Many are married, sometimes sharing their enjoyment of female dress with understanding wives.

"Janice" is a lifelong heterosexual transvestite man whose desire to be a woman has become so strong over the years that at forty-nine he is about to undergo a sex-change operation. As George he still works as a barber, but as Janice, in wig, makeup, and stylish clothes, "she" has a second job as a motel manager. Most of Janice's friends and coworkers know that she is not a 100 percent female yet, but George will be out of a job when the surgical changes are made. Janice has undergone hormone treatments and therapy for a year to prepare for the final changeover, making her at present a preoperative transsexual. Her body now has a woman's contours, and she loves the clothes that go with it. A hundred and twenty dresses, eighty pairs of shoes, twenty-two wigs, diamonds, furs, and a Cadillac are part of her new self-image. As Janice told us, "Poor George's been working his butt off and Janice's been spending it."

George's wife of fifteen years could never reconcile herself to her husband's alternate identity, but their two children have accepted Janice without apparent difficulty. They love this parent and are glad that the change will bring her peace of mind after years of torment. Unlike Bud, who has always believed that one must find the strength to accept one's lot and make the best of it, Janice feels that her only alternatives were self-mutilation or suicide.

The confusion of gays with transsexuals and transvestites leads to a popular myth that as homosexuality becomes increasingly accepted, gay men will begin coming to work in dresses and high heels, or makeup and padded bras. This fear is utterly without foundation. We have attended many gay functions; we frequent gay bars, clubs, church services, and dances, and the only ones we see in "drag" are the self-identified, acknowledged transvestites and preoperative transsexuals. The vast majority of gay men would feel ridiculous in women's attire and would not adopt it if they could.

We once asked a middle-aged gay gentleman, impeccably groomed in sport coat and dark trousers, what he would like to wear to a cocktail party if he had a choice. He told us that a fur-trimmed caftan would be his preference. This costume was traditional for prosperous and portly Renaissance men and conforms well to the mature male physique; we hope to see him in one before too long.

So far, we've been using the words *heterosexual, homosexual, gay,* and *straight* as if they meant something precise that we can all agree on. In fact, these terms are convenient simplifications for the idea that most people engage in sexual relations with only one sex. To get a clearer perspective on the part homosexual behavior plays in the total range of American sexual experience, we should first take a look at *bisexuality* to evaluate its significance in the gay (and straight) world.

There are certainly far more individuals with bisexual experience than there are lifelong exclusive homosexuals. We know of one woman who is happily married but has recently fallen in love and is having an affair with another woman. We also know a married man who regularly dates both men and women. He and his wife have an open marriage, and she has always known about his bisexual interests. Many men whose wives are not so broad-minded either pick up occasional lovers in the homosexual cruising areas of large cities or indulge this preference on out-of-town business trips.

Sexual identity is usually fixed early in life, but some people feel different at different times. A large group of bisexual women reported in a *Ms.* magazine article* that when they fell in love it was with a person rather than a gender; one woman described herself as being homosexual or heterosexual depending on the person she happened to be involved with at the moment.

In our society women are generally less threatened than men by the knowledge that they are capable of homosexual love, perhaps because more men in our culture fear sexual inadequacy and associate a homosexual orientation with effeminacy. Consider Michael, for instance. Now almost forty, he has been divorced for ten years and has two children. Since that time he has had affairs with dozens of different women and is still looking for one with whom he can be physically and emotionally comfortable for more than a few weeks at a time. Michael knows that he is strongly attracted to men but says he would not be able to cope with a gay experience. He hopes that somewhere, sometime, he will meet the woman who can meet his needs; the possibility that she might turn out to be a man is so upsetting that he refuses to think about it.

Predominantly gay men and women may also engage in heterosexual relations, often for personal reasons that transcend sexual preference. Bob, who works as a secretary for a management consulting firm, has been gay all his life. For ten years he had a male lover, but since they broke up Bob has been making as many contacts with men as he can. It's difficult, because he doesn't have much money and he's shy. Bob sees a woman friend regularly and she doesn't object when he visits gay bars on the vacation trips they occasionally take together. Now and then he sleeps with her, more or less as a gesture of friendship. This kind of sex is OK, he says, though the excitement he feels with men is missing.

* *Ms.* magazine, November 1976.

Evelyn, a black woman in her late twenties, talks about her sexual orientation this way:

I guess you'd call me bisexual but I'm really mostly gay. But I go out with guys once in a while. Just most of my real loves have been girls. There's one guy I see now; we go out once in a while, sometimes have sex. But when I'm really in love I don't bother with anybody else. I've only been in love with one guy, and I married him. That was when I was young—just a kid really—sixteen. He and I split up after a couple of years and a couple of kids. He ran around too much. We were just young.

When I was a little kid I felt sexy toward everybody. It wasn't until high school that I thought there was anything different about being turned on to girls. I started hearing lezzie jokes and it dawned on me that there was a name for me. I was glad when my husband and I got it on so well, 'cause then I didn't have to worry about it, but I never for a minute gave up wanting girls, even when I was madly in love with James. I didn't especially want to do anything about it, but I always knew I was gay underneath. It just seems to me to be the most natural thing to be. I can't see myself only turned on to men. I just can't imagine it. It's like leaving half the world out.

The first comprehensive report on sexual orientation among Americans was done by Dr. Alfred Kinsey and his coworkers at the Institute for Sex Research in Bloomington, Indiana. A volume covering male practices appeared in 1948 and a second one devoted to sexuality among women was published in 1953. Some of the most startling statistics, which were much quoted though not widely believed at that time, showed that more than one-third of American males between the ages of sixteen and fifty-five had experienced sexual arousal to orgasm with another man at least once. Dr. Kinsey and his colleagues had interviewed twelve thousand men to arrive at his sexual profiles.

The research team made no effort to classify men as "heterosexual" or "homosexual." Instead, they developed a scale on the basis of overt sexual experience plus noncontact or "psychic" arousal.

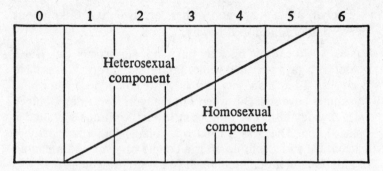

Heterosexual-homosexual component scale

Based on overt experience plus degree of psychic arousal, any individual falls into one of seven categories as follows:

0. Exclusively heterosexual arousal and experience. No homosexual component.
1. Predominance of heterosexual arousal and experience. Incidental homosexual arousal and/or experience.
2. Largely heterosexual orientation. Some significant degree of homosexual arousal and/or experience.
3. Equal homo- and heterosexual arousal and experience. •
4. As for 2 (above), but with sexual orientation reversed.
5. As for 1 (above), but with sexual orientation reversed.
6. Exclusively homosexual arousal and experience.

Thus, a woman or man who has had incidental homosexual experiences with a friend during high school, or who has been occasionally attracted to someone of the same sex, would be classified as a 1 on the scale. The man who has a mutually satisfying relationship with his wife but whose history includes occasional homosexual adventures (sometimes known as the "God-was-I-drunk-last-night-I-don't-remember-a-thing!" syndrome) might be classified as a 2. Our friend Jeff, who claims that attractive men and attractive women interest him equally, falls into the 3 category, whereas Elizabeth, who knows that she likes women better even though sex with her husband can be fun, too, could be considered a 4. The majority of gays who have tried heterosexual relationships but never really found them satisfying are probably 5's. Only a person who has never been aroused by the opposite sex can be classified as a 6; according to Institute for Sex Research studies on homosexuality, this category includes only about 4 percent of American males.

Dr. Kinsey and his colleagues selected some of their survey results as being particularly helpful in demonstrating the prevalence of homosexual behavior and interest among American men. Their data were later criticized by some professionals on the grounds that the survey sample included an unduly large number of prison inmates, but recent research confirms their basic validity. We show some of their results here, to emphasize the large numbers of men who rate above 0 on the heterosexual-homosexual component scale.

- Three out of eight men have some homosexual experience resulting in orgasm during or after adolescence.
- Half of the men who remain single until their mid-thirties have had such experiences.
- One out of eight men experiences erotic reaction to other males *in the absence* of any overt homosexual experience after adolescence.
- Almost one man in five has a rating of 3 or above on the scale during a period of three years or more past the age of fifteen.
- One man in eight has a rating of 4 or above during such a period.

- One man out of twelve rates 5 or above on the scale during a period of at least three years past the age of fifteen.

The Kinsey team studied certain sociological factors, such as urban versus rural background, importance of religion in the life of each person surveyed, and educational level, to see whether such factors were significantly related to amount of homosexual behavior. The only obvious correlative factor was educational level: persons with only a grade school education practiced more than average homosexuality; high school graduates practiced homosexuality least; and college-level individuals were in between but closer to the grade school men. The assumption is that better-educated people are more adventurous and less fearful of deviating from the norm than the average high school graduate. Lower-socioeconomic-level males, on the other hand, have little to lose in terms of reputation, social position, high-status jobs, and such.

In their study of female sexual behavior,* Dr. Kinsey and his team avoided including an undue proportion of prison inmates; consequently their figures for women are considered to have been quite valid. About eight thousand women were surveyed. By thirty years of age, homosexual experience to the point of orgasm had occurred in 6 percent of grade school graduates, 5 percent of the high school sample, 10 percent of college women, and 14 percent of those who had attended graduate school.† Between 11 and 20 percent of unmarried women, 8 and 10 percent of wives, and 14 and 17 percent of previously married women received ratings at the 1 level or higher. Rated anywhere from 2 to 6 were 6 to 14 percent of unmarried, 2 to 3 percent of married, and 8 to 10 percent of previously married women. In the 3 to 6 category, the figures were 4 to 11 percent, 1 to 2

---

* Indiana University, Institute for Sex Research, *Sexual Behavior in the Human Female* (Philadelphia: W. B. Saunders, 1953), p. 842.
† Ibid., pp. 459–60.

percent, and 5 to 7 percent respectively. Rated 4 to 6 (predominantly homosexual in preference) were 3 to 8 percent of unmarried, less than 1 percent of married, and 4 to 7 percent of previously married women. A sizable number of women (14 to 19 percent of unmarried, 1 to 3 percent of married, and 5 to 8 percent of previously married) had never been aroused sexually by another person, male or female.*

We find, in talking to nongay people about homosexuality, that there is an enormous interest in what actually goes on in bed. We could summarize the whole subject by saying that gay men do all the things men everywhere either do or would like to do, and women offer each other all the things that women everywhere like or would like to have done to them. In most cases, lovers take turns being the active or passive partner, but of course no hard and fast rules exist about who does what to whom—it's a matter of individual preference. There is no way we can describe everybody's love life because infinite possibilities for variety exist, all of them doubtless practiced with vigor and enthusiasm by any number of people.

But we can try, for the sake of parents who want to know, to be a little more specific. In general, men tend to enjoy a direct genital approach. They commonly like to get down to business right away, and they can often be aroused by the prospect of sex with any number of other interested males. Some men prefer to act as receptors for sexual acts and are turned on only by highly masculine types. Others, including a high percentage of men who do not consider themselves to be gay, prefer the aggressor or "inserter" role. Oral sex and mutual masturbation can be as important as, or more important than, anal intercourse, depending again on individual preference.

By and large, gay women tend to be less promiscuous

* Ibid., pp. 472–74.

than gay men. Joanie's remarks are typical: "It's where a woman's head is at—it's all in the head. A woman is less physical than a man. I have to like somebody very much to get turned on. I've tried picking up women in bars—messing around—but it's too awkward. We didn't know each other well enough."

Women like to be stroked, caressed, fondled. Again, some are more aggressive and some more passive, but lovers generally enjoy taking turns. Often the more experienced partner teaches the less knowledgeable one how to explore and stimulate all parts of the body to mutual satisfaction. The best lovemaking can be a long-drawn-out, leisurely process of slowly mounting excitement, since women generally become aroused more slowly than men and are capable of sustaining a state of desire over a long period of time. They also have the capacity for multiple orgasms. Several studies, including the Kinsey report, show that women bring each other to orgasm more effectively than a man can usually do.

Both men and women, even though they may sometimes be able to enjoy making love with members of the opposite sex, are fervent about the emotional high that they experience in homosexual love. There's an involvement of the mind and spirit as well as the body. Tom says he is occasionally attracted to women, but the first time he ever kissed a man he knew he was glad to be gay. He was twenty then, and the feeling of excitement was a complete surprise: "That may not sound surprising, but it was to me. It took the whole idea of sexuality beyond the limits of physical experience."

In terms of sexual development, it is generally assumed that "normal" people have a capacity to become sexually aroused only by the opposite sex, and that sexual urges do not manifest themselves until sometime in late adolescence. But this theory is considered by many experts to be based more on what we have been taught about "appropriate" sexuality than on how people really behave.

Babies are sexual beings. They love to be caressed and held, not only for warmth and security, but because it feels good to their bodies. When they play with their genitals, the pleasant sensation is part of a generalized sensuality that only later becomes focused as genital sexuality. Young children play with their own and each other's bodies because it is a pleasurable activity, the more interesting in our culture for being illicit.

Almost all boys engage in masturbation, and most in mutual sex play. Eighty-eight percent of males masturbate by the age of thirteen or older, according to the statistics compiled by Dr. Kinsey and his associates, and 70 percent report some experience with mutual displays of sexuality, commonly between the ages of eight and thirteen. Usually this takes place in the company of other boys rather than girls, in part because of the social taboos against heterosexual experimentation. Almost all boys are interested in their own and other males' genitalia, but homosexually inclined individuals evidently feel strong sexual impulses at an earlier age. They masturbate at an earlier age and more frequently, and are more likely to be aware of erotic impulses directed toward individuals, usually boys of their own age, but often toward older men. It is not true that most homosexual initiation comes through seduction by an older man; very often the reverse is true. Dr. Franklin Kameny of Washington, D.C.'s, Mattachine Society tells us that he frequently takes calls from boys seeking advice on how to seduce an older man. However, 81 percent of gay men reported to Dr. Kinsey's team that their first homosexual arousal was a genital contact with another boy.

Bobby Graetz, writing in *Changes,* a collection of articles by young homosexuals in Howard County, Maryland, describes his early feelings this way:

I have been aware of my attraction for men most of my life. Like most people, I had homosexual experiences when I was first becoming aware of my sexuality. My first experience occurred when I was in the sixth grade. I felt different from the other boys I had sex with though. They would always talk about the girls they wanted to go to bed with. They saw their homosexuality as a phase, and that they would move up to better things, in other words, females. I would nod my head and try to be interested in the conversation, but I didn't want to have sex with girls. I was very excited about my friends' bodies, and really got off having sex with them. I always felt that I would grow out of it and become interested in the opposite sex someday. I kept on waiting but the day never came.

I had fantasies about being picked up by homosexuals but it never happened to me. I was very disappointed because the only way I would get my sexual needs met was through someone else's initiation. I was too frightened by others' reactions if I were to make the first move.

For women, early sexual awareness most often means romantic attachments, "crushes" on other girls or older women. Glenda, a twenty-seven-year-old lawyer, tells a typical story:

In fifth grade I had a crush on a friend of mine. I'd buy her things, wanted to be with her all the time. Then in sixth grade I had a crush on another girl 'cause she said I was cute. I remember having sexual feelings about her. Then in seventh grade I had a recurring dream about a friend of mine. She was my best friend. I really loved her; she was so beautiful and her laugh just made me melt inside. In the dream we would make love, and I don't know how I even knew about how women made love, I'd never heard about it or read any books, but there it was in the dreams. I got scared of feeling this way, afraid she'd find out and be offended, that I'd say the wrong thing and be rejected, so I broke off the relationship with her.

Delores, who is twenty-six, remembers vividly having a crush on an older woman. Although she says that she knew then that she would always love women, we ought not to forget that many straight women have had this childhood experience; we might say that a childhood crush, or a series of them, merely means that a woman rates a "1" or more on the Kinsey scale. Delores says:

I knew I was gay in second grade. I had the biggest crush on my teacher. Once I heard her say she liked people who didn't wear glasses, so even though I needed glasses I didn't wear them, trying to get her to like me. That was a huge crush. A couple of years later I heard she was getting married, so I called her up to tell her how happy I was for her. She didn't even remember who I was, and she must have thought it was crazy, but I still had that crush on her.

I started having relationships when I was eleven or twelve. My mother's best friend's niece and I used to play together and we had a physical relationship. Neither of us knew what we were doing. That lasted three years. Then there was another family we knew in T., and the girl and I had a relationship that lasted for four years. Both those girls were around my age. In high school I didn't have any relationships. My friends would all be going on dates and they'd try to get me to get a date and come with them, but I just wouldn't do it. I'd go out with them sometimes, but alone, and just sit there and watch them. My emotional relationships with girls then were good, but no physical relationships. I hadn't put words to what I was then; I thought it seemed natural, but then I noticed I was different. There were two girls in my school and there were rumors that they were "funny"; that's what they called it, but I just steered clear of them.

Almost all girls who have crushes feel a desire to protect or "do things for" the loved one, but the girls who later come out as gays are also frequently aware of having wanted bodily contact such as kissing or touching. In contrast to gay men, the earliest recognizably lesbian sexual arousal is usually caused by some casual contact such as holding hands or sleeping in the same bed, less frequently as a result of hugging or kissing, and least commonly (25 percent) by genital contacts.* A majority of gay women (and many straight women as well) recall having experienced homoerotic arousal or sex play with other girls before the age of

* Saghir, Marcel T., and Robins, Eli, *Male and Female Homosexuality: A Comprehensive Investigation* (Baltimore: The Williams & Wilkins Company, 1973), p. 210.

fourteen, whereas initial heterosexual attraction seems generally to occur at a later age. Masturbation is more common among lesbians (80 percent) than among straight women (45 percent).* Most gay women also report a history of some degree of sexual attraction to men, particularly prior to their self-discovery as lesbians.

It is important to emphasize that a large percentage of lesbian women really are not aware of homosexual desires when they are young or else don't understand their significance. Over and over again we hear, "When I was younger I didn't really know I was a lesbian, I just knew I was different." Glenda has this to say:

In high school I had a string of guys. We'd kiss and I started enjoying that but I didn't want intercourse and I thought there was something wrong with me. So at seventeen I did it to see what was supposed to be so wonderful and it was just blah, nothing compared to those dreams! But I got pregnant. Later I got to enjoy sex with men, but there was always something missing; no matter how good it was, I knew there was something of myself I was repressing. Now I don't relate at all to men sexually.

Sometimes girls who have had a history of childhood and adolescent crushes on women experience their first sexual desires with men, as reported by Peggy, a thirty-eight-year-old writer. She had never had directly sexual fantasies about women, just strong feelings of "wanting to be friends."

My first sexual experiences were dancing and necking with boys. I don't remember an overwhelming sense of sexuality until I was a senior in high school, when we had these heavy necking parties. I was pretty naive sexually. So it wasn't a problem, except later, around the marriage thing, focusing on one man, and what happens to all your friends. It seemed strange, but I figured, well, when I'm ready for it, I'll go through the change and I'll be ready for it. And that's what I never did.

* Ibid., p. 216.

Generally speaking, gay men have a pretty good idea that they are "different" at least by adolescence and sometimes long before. In many cases they do everything they can to deny their sexuality. Jim, a physician in a large eastern city, comes from an Italian Catholic family. During high school, college, medical school, and internship he "just lived celibate," hoping that he could resist his homosexual desires, that there would never be any "incidents." Then, after his first experience, at twenty-seven, he "hoped it would never happen again" and that he would begin to desire women. He was twenty-nine before he accepted gay identity, and then with great reluctance.

Women, on the other hand, often reach adulthood and marriage before they have any idea at all of wanting sex with other women. Joanie was engaged twice and had had numerous lovers by the time she was twenty-two, but had always felt that going to bed with a man was somehow "out of character." She had close women friends in college and enjoyed drawing female nudes in art class, but had never thought of going to bed with a woman except perhaps as a "lark." One night, though, she went to a gay bar and met Kathy; they went home together. "One day I was straight and the next day I was gay. It was what I had been looking for, only I didn't know it. You're either gay or you're straight, nobody can convert you. But if I were in a situation where there were no attractive women around, I could consider going back to men."

As a matter of fact, she and Kathy broke up after two and a half years and for a while Joanie did consider going back to a previous boyfriend. Now twenty-eight, she has been living with exclusively homosexual Pat for a year and considers herself extremely happy.

There have not as yet been any definitive studies of how sexual orientation develops. Hormone deficiency or an over-supply of the wrong hormone is *not* characteristic of homosexually inclined persons. Everyone has a mixture of male and female hormones, with male sex organs producing more testosterone than estrogen, and female organs the reverse. More testosterone in your system makes you more sexually aggressive and more estrogen more passive, that is, ready to accept sexual advances from someone else. Neither causes a change in the object of sexual desire, whether it be male or female.

No one theory of causation seems to fit all cases, though any one may have some relevance in the development of a particular individual. One theory that makes some sense to us was explained by an anthropology professor. He points out that in all higher mammals and in almost every known human population, homosexual behavior appears as a *recurrent trait.* That is to say, a certain percentage of individuals turn out to have homosexual preference no matter what their cultural conditioning may be. Whatever genetic factors may be involved here are not transmitted through a population the way blue eyes or curly hair or sickle-cell anemia are. In other words, gayness doesn't run in families, though of course we do know families in which more than one person is gay.

It seems probable that none of us is born with fixed sexual orientation. We learn it. *Gender identity* (knowing oneself to be a male or female) is evidently established about the time a person learns to talk. *Sexual orientation,* or determination of sexual object choice, on the other hand, seems in many cases to be closely related to acceptance or rejection of the role one is expected to play in society as a man or a woman. It is generally felt to be fixed by the time a child starts school, if not sooner. If a boy is comfortable with the idea of playing the role that he perceives as appropriate for males, he is probably more likely to direct his developing sexuality toward females, given the assumption that at birth he has no fixed sexual orientation. That assumption may in fact be open to question, as we shall see later. But for the moment, how do most of us learn to direct our sexuality toward the opposite rather than the same sex? How do we learn to define ourselves as sexual people? And what function do older male and female role models play in this process?

There is a lot of confusion in people's minds concerning the matter of role models, including a widespread misconception that the presence of homosexual people in a child's environment can cause homosexuality, as if it were catching, like measles. One hears a lot of talk about homosexuals "recruiting" children, for example. This concept misses the point. Virtually all children grow up in heterosexual homes, knowing nothing about gays or gay life; direct heterosexual programming begins almost at birth.

So how does conditioning work or, perhaps, fail? One line of reasoning has it that if a boy sees himself as an inadequate male or a girl does not feel that she fits the pattern of a successful woman, physical desire for the opposite sex is rejected because it seems to be an unreachable goal, and the child turns instead to members of the same sex for gratification. This is said to happen in families where the mother is dominant or overprotective and the father harsh, remote, or absent, causing a male child to identify with the mother.

According to Dr. Wardell Pomeroy, joint author of the Kinsey reports, 85 percent of gay men do come from such families, but so do 50 to 60 percent of straight men.* Don, who is forty-two years old and lost both parents as a child, tends to agree with the dominant-female theory. He himself was raised by a grandmother and a single uncle, who he says was not gay. "Every gay male that I've met had a domineering mother or a compliant or nonexistent father. Dominant, not necessarily domineering. My grandmother laid down the law; she said what the rules were."

Larry, Don's lover, disagrees. In his family both parents arrive at a decision together. And Joe, who is twenty-eight

* Fast, Julius, and Wells, Hal, *Bisexual Living* (New York: Pocket Books, 1975), p. 254.

and comes from a small town in New Jersey, observes that his father had a strong positive influence on his childhood. "I don't believe that there was any dominance in our family. My parents never really did anything together; they acted as two individuals. My father and I were the only ones in the family group [four children] that had any kind of a relationship since we were always out on weekends, going camping and bird-watching."

Certainly not all lesbians have domineering fathers and weak or absent mothers; quite the contrary. Cheryl, who is a twenty-four-year-old black woman, made the following remarks about her relationship with her father:

My father and I were always real close. He didn't live with us; he'd come around every few weeks and I just adored him. He died when I was nineteen and I still miss that man. He'd do anything for me. That's one thing that always bothered me, that he wouldn't have liked me being gay. I think he would have thought I let him down. He would always tell me how pretty I was and how I'd be driving the boys wild someday. He meant well and I wouldn't want to hurt him, so maybe it's just as well he's gone.

One study* tries to demonstrate that lesbians (as compared to straight women) are twice as likely to have dominating mothers and that they either were intimate with their fathers or had no father at all, none of which makes much sense to us somehow. However, we do think it likely that some mothers have difficulty relating to their gay daughters, and that the resulting conflicts might well be perceived by the daughter as an effort to dominate. Another theory has it that if a child receives strong emotional support from the opposite-sex parent, and if that support is suddenly withdrawn before the end of the child's formative years, the resulting loss of faith in that parent will prevent the child from ever again daring to become emotionally dependent on a person of the opposite sex.

But it's a mistake to think that all gay people come from

* Saghir and Robins, *Male and Female Homosexuality*, p. 301.

troubled families. Grace, for example, who is twenty-two and an only child, says, "My parents are devoted to each other; they gave me a lot of love. I don't see any clear-cut roles between Mom and Dad. My father works in the garden, my mother I guess does most of the cooking, but it's an equal relationship."

The majority of gays with whom we talk either tell us that they think they were "born that way" or that the subject of causation is irrelevant. Ed, who is twenty-two, takes the latter position. "I really don't think there's much need to find out what makes people gay or straight. It's something that's been going on ever since the dawn of recorded history and will be going on when the world as we know it ceases to exist. It's a natural phenomenon and natural phenomena can't, or shouldn't, be tampered with."

Walter, forty-one, has this to say: "When you're brought up in the straight world and you're a young gay, you think it's just not natural, but what can you do about it? As far as I was concerned, I was born that way. I guess I realized when I was three years old when I was playing with the boy next door and he was playing with me. I don't think my mother made me gay, nor do I think my father made me gay."

Charlie, who is twenty, was raised in a small town in Illinois and now attends a prominent Jesuit university. Perhaps he states the case best for a lot of gay men and women: "I think it's a waste of time [looking for causes]. It doesn't bother me. I'm not concerned with how I came to be gay. I think when you're looking for a cause, then you're viewing it as an illness; that really bothers me."

There are no simple answers. Almost anyone might grow up to be almost anything, within some broad, possibly genetically determined range. Most people, for instance, are probably genetically capable of developing a sexual orientation anywhere from 0 to 4 on the Kinsey scale, whereas others might have a potential of 1 to 6, and some might be limited to the 3 to 6 range. Peggy, quoted earlier, agrees with us: "I think everybody is potentially bisexual and certain conditions push you one way or the other. Most of the conditions in this society push you toward heterosexuality."

Possibly there are some crucial stages of development when a variety of factors might interfere with the usual male-female conditioning process. Such key stages appear most likely to occur within the first five or six years of life, but sexual orientation can perhaps be modified at later crucial periods in certain cases.

Peter, who is twenty-eight and went through a divorce before coming to grips with his sexual preference, has this to say: "I think it's just there, it's something that if parents look to destroy it, it makes it worse. If the child is allowed to develop naturally, if the parents can help develop whatever the child picks up on, I think that would save a lot of frustration. Sexual preferences, tendencies, whatever, 90 percent of it is in the mind."

We think that Peter, who, incidentally, has only a high school education and is in no way an intellectual, has hit on the crux of the issue. As parents, we all raise our children in the best way we know. At some indefinable point in time, probably very early in most cases, the personality takes shape. Some of it's nature, some of it's nurture. Who knows whether Billy has a moody disposition because he takes after his grandfather, or because his parents frustrated him, or because he just happens to have a moody disposition? Trying to tamper with a child's personality just drives him underground, or makes him feel inadequate, or both. As long as he seems to be happy and he's not harming anyone else, we're in favor of letting him develop in the way that seems right to him. And we musn't forget to let him know that he's the best Billy we'll ever have.

Many of us parents are anxious to know how we can tell if our child is going to be gay. The answer is, we can't. No one is able to predict how a particular child will turn out based on early childhood behavior or influences. One indicator of sexual object choice, though, is sometimes thought to be found in the childhood tomboy/sissy syndrome. Not every tomboy turns out to be a lesbian, nor is every sissy boy growing up gay; even among adults, we all know mannish women and effeminate men who are 100 percent heterosexual. A very feminine little girl may come to prefer females as companions and lovers, and any number of gay men are extremely masculine in manner and appearance.

Nevertheless, Saghir and Robin* report that two-thirds of gay men had been perceived as sissies in childhood. This was not due to any physical differences from other boys, but rather to their failure or unwillingness to play whatever role was considered appropriate for boys in their community. The sissy boys were teased by other boys and often rejected by their fathers as well, often weakening their self-image and injecting them with negative feelings about homosexuality, making self-acceptance as gay more difficult later on. A boy who is uneasy about his image as a male because of parental or peer rejection may even be fostering a homosexual identity. We know many gay men who believe that their homosexual interests derive from an idealization of males who seemed to fit that image better than they themselves did.

Seventy percent of lesbians but only 16 percent of straight women in one study† reported that they or others regarded them as tomboys in childhood, although being a tomboy is not as shameful as being a sissy. A majority of lesbian tomboys wished at one time to be males, usually because boys' lives seemed to offer more status and freedom, but sometimes because they wanted to be able to make love to girls. Anne, a twenty-three-year-old black woman, told us that she used to want to be a boy.

Growing up, I always liked to be on my own. I liked to climb trees; I was what you'd call then a tomboy. For a time, when I

---

* *Male and Female Homosexuality*, pp. 18–21.
† Ibid., p. 193.

got to be around eleven, my mother started trying to change my ways. She had never really discouraged my liking to wear jeans and be alone and run and play with the boys, and suddenly she said I had to act different now. I was growing up, too old for that. Then she explained about being a woman, menstruation, that I had to act like a lady. It didn't make any sense. I noticed other girls were doing the same thing; all of a sudden we couldn't play with the boys, or do rough sports; most of us really resented it. So I thought it was better to be a boy; they got to do everything I wanted to do. I started to resent being a girl, and didn't want to mature, because breasts seemed like something of a disadvantage. I wouldn't have wanted to be a boy if they didn't put such restrictions on being a girl. I didn't want to have a boy's body; I didn't want a penis, I wanted to be me, and it seemed that boys got to be themselves and girls had to act funny and make believe and not show their true feelings, especially around boys. The separation got very clear. Girls could act like people with other girl friends, but being with a boy was an act. We were taught to act ladylike, not fight or be aggressive. What was accepted as natural in a boy was bad manners for a girl. I refused to accept this. My parents decided to send me to a psychiatrist to help me adjust to being a woman. By then I already knew I had some sexual feelings for other girls my age.

A minority of male gays report that they ever wanted to be women. (This may tell us more about American cultural values than it does about the homosexual condition.) Of course there are exceptions, and George is one of them: "The only thing that I remember . . . is that I wanted to be a female. I think, looking at that, it wasn't that I really wanted to be, because I have no desire to be today, but I think I must have had a sexual attraction to men and I must have started to feel some of the social pressures that this is a no-no, and I think that's why I wanted to be a woman at that early age [prepuberty]."

Healthy gay men and women consider their sexual orientation to be an asset rather than a disadvantage. A gay man is free in ways that a man identified as straight usually cannot permit himself to be. He feels free to see other men as potential lovers, rather than as competitors against whom he must measure his achievements and values. And he often feels that his sexual role can let him be more tender, compassionate, supportive, emotional, sensitive, and uninhibited. On the other hand, he is also free to be tough, stoical, aggressive, and to define himself as a man's man in a world where masculine qualities and male beauty represent the ideal. In short, a gay man can be as "manly" or as "feminine" as his nature dictates. There is no preconceived mold for a gay man, unless he chooses to adopt the popular stereotype of being effeminate and mannered. He makes his own mold, as indeed we all must if we are to be truly free.

Gay women can be strong, determined, aggressive, competitive, if that is their nature. They may also be delicate, yielding, shy, completely "feminine" in looks and manner. A lesbian can seek mates freely, rather than having to program herself to be sought after. She can live her private life in an all-female world and know that for her it is a complete world. She earns her place by exercising her own capabilities, and not by seeing herself as Mrs. Somebody Important, or Mrs. Nobody Special, or, worst of all, Miss Couldn't Get One. Gay women are free to enjoy individual men as colleagues, friends, even occasionally as lovers, not as prizes to be won in competition against others of her own sex. Feminine beauty is a lesbian woman's ideal—she identifies with womanliness as a political, emotional, and spiritual state of being.

These are woman-loving women, sisters who support sisters. They feel that they are free to express their true female potential—caring, supporting, giving pleasure to one who feels exactly the same way they do and understands them better than a man ever could. A lesbian writer once put it: "Most people's ideas about lesbianism come from pornographic films and magazines, all of which are pro-

duced by and for men. . . . Men who are obsessed with sex
are convinced that Lesbians are obsessed with sex. Actually, like other women, Lesbians are obsessed with love and
fidelity."*

Gay people of both sexes know that positive gay identity
is a rich gift, achieved in spite of terrifying social opposition, and they respect and admire one another for continually struggling to maintain it. Listen to Marilyn, forty-one
years old, whose conversation we taped during a recent
interview. She was responding to the question "Why are you
glad to be gay?"

Well, just because of how much I love Ann. You know, she
makes me so happy that I can't think of not loving her and she's
a woman and that makes me gay. She really knows me, she
knows me like no man ever could; even the nicest man would
never be like me in the same way a woman is. Also, sometimes
I look around Sappho's [a women's bar] and see all these great
women having a good time with each other, laughing and talking, so many different kinds of women, rich and poor, grungy-
looking and fancy, black and white, and I think, this couldn't
happen anywhere but in a gay bar.

I've always been gay, so it's hard to think what I like about
it. I just like me, so I like what I am, which is gay. One good
thing that happened at work was when my friend Sandy told me
she was proud of me for being gay, that she wished she had
the nerve, 'cause she can see how happy I am. That made me
feel great.

When I was younger, I didn't really know I was a lesbian, I
just knew I was different. Now with all the gay pride and
women's lib I feel like I'm not alone, like there's a whole bunch
of people who think I'm great, just for being the way I am. I'm
glad I'm gay because there are so many beautiful women around
and I like them and they like me. . . . When I hear people say
they wouldn't want to be gay because it's such a lonely life, I
just laugh. Now I'm not saying there aren't lonely gay people.

* *Woman, a Journal of Liberation*, vol. 1, no. 4, 1970, p. 36.

What Is Gay?

Everyone is lonely sometimes, but as a way of life which would you rather, to be part of a group of great people who stick by each other and love each other, with sex as well as without it, or be tied perhaps to one man who thinks he's better than you, with hardly a chance to have close friends 'cause you're always cleaning up after him, worrying that you'll lose him and be out on the street? So I ask you, who's lonely?

Making Their Way
in the World

The following resolution was adopted as the policy of the American Federation of Teachers by the AFT Executive Council in 1970:

> Discrimination Against Homosexuals Denounced
>
> Whereas, professional people insist that they be judged on the basis of professional and not personal criteria; and
>
> Whereas, it is the responsibility of trade unions to provide job protection from all forms of discrimination that is not based on performance such as race, color, sex, religion, age, or ethnic origin; be it
>
> Resolved, that the American Federation of Teachers protests any personnel actions taken against any teacher merely because he or she practices homosexual behavior in private life.

OK. You know your child is gay, and you know what it means that he or she is gay. Your next worry is your concern for your child's future. Will she still have a job? Will he still succeed?

The answer is, of course, if she wants to, if he wants to, they will. But, as always, there are many factors to consider.

As with every other aspect of gay life, where you live is probably the biggest factor in the degree of job equality you can expect. In New York City, San Francisco, Chicago, Los Angeles, the chances are that no one in a large company is going to know or care what you do after hours. Gays are everywhere, and everyone is used to having them around. You can be open or not, whatever makes you more comfortable. In small towns, in southern states, in strongly religious communities, watch out unless you've got thick skin and something to live on while you look for a job.

Some types of work you can forget unless you are willing to stay in the closet, and except in cities where by law all municipal jobs are awarded irrespective of sexual preference, the most obvious of these is teaching. There is no field of employment in which fear of homosexuality is more pervasive or more emotionally loaded. The subject of whether exposure to gay men and women in classrooms and locker rooms encourages homosexuality in students is hardly ever debated publicly, and in the few instances where this happens, more heat than light is usually generated. In most parts of this country, gay schoolteachers lie as low as possible. A friend of ours who has been a school librarian for nearly twenty years tells us that she only came out once to another teacher in all that time. She has no idea of whether any of her fellow teachers are gay. She has never discussed homosexuality with any student. Known gay teachers in her home state have been fired out of hand and barred from practicing their profession thereafter, and few others care to undergo that risk.

Joe Acanfora's experience is a case in point. He was a student teacher in the State College, Pennsylvania, school system when school officials read in the newspapers that he and others were suing Penn State University to gain official recognition for a student gay rights organization. Joe was dismissed from his student teaching program immediately and was forbidden to enter the school building. After considerable publicity, he regained his appointment by court order and received excellent evaluations at the completion of his teaching assignment. A panel of six deans from the university questioned him about his sex life for two hours before splitting three to three on whether to recommend him for certification as a teacher in Pennsylvania. The state secretary of education finally decided to certify him in September 1972.

Meanwhile, Joe had accepted a position in Montgomery County, Maryland, to teach eighth-grade earth science. When newspaper accounts of the Pennsylvania certification decision reached his employers, they transferred him to their curriculum department because "that does not require contact with youngsters." His contract was not renewed for the next school year.

Joe is a mild-mannered and soft-spoken young man, but he is also a fighter. The National Education Association backed him in a series of lawsuits to gain reinstatement. A U.S. district court ruled the following year that knowledge of a teacher's homosexuality does not constitute grounds for dismissal, but decided against his suit because he had "shown an indifference to the bounds of propriety" by discussing the case on CBS's *60 Minutes* and WNET's *How Do Your Children Grow?* This rationale was dismissed by the U.S. Fourth Circuit Court of Appeals, but it nonetheless upheld Montgomery County on the grounds that Joe had failed to list his membership in gay activist organizations on his employment application.

Joe is no longer teaching earth science, or anything else, for that matter; but he is continuing to work on behalf of gay rights on a national scale. That movement, in our opinion, is fortunate to have him, for he is an imaginative and decisive leader. Montgomery County's children, however, have lost a competent and dedicated science teacher.

Why was Mr. Acanfora such a threat to eight-grade students? Child molestation has proved to be pretty much of a dead issue. A large proportion of homosexual offenses are perpetrated by mentally ill men who have also molested females at one time or another. At least 75 percent of these sex criminals have heterosexual histories and 50 percent are married. And two-thirds have turned out to be older friends of their victims or family members.

It has been estimated that six thousand to ten thousand gays teach New York City school children, yet between 1930 and 1970 there was only one case of homosexual molestation. During the same period, however, many teachers were accused of improper involvement with a student of the opposite sex. In 1976 the school board's personnel director assured a Gay Teachers Association forum that gays "have the same rights and privileges as any other teacher in the system." A teacher's private life is not a "bar to entrance into teaching in New York City nor to the continuance of teaching." He urged teachers who feel that they are being harassed because of their sexual preference to call on him personally for help.

The Acanfora case produced quantities of expert testimony regarding the suitability of homosexual teachers as role models for school-aged youngsters. The *Washington Post* ran the following statements in an article dated April 15, 1973:

Dr. William R. Stayton, psychologist and sex counselor at the University of Pennsylvania School of Medicine, testified that the teacher's presence in the junior high school classroom would be beneficial to heterosexually inclined boys in "breaking down homosexual stereotypes" and would "affirm the self-image of that small minority of homosexually inclined boys."

Stayton and Dr. Stanford B. Friedman, pediatrician and professor of psychiatry at the University of Rochester School of Medicine, agreed that Acanfora would not influence his teen-age students to become homosexuals. [They] testified ... that contrary to popular assumption, youngsters by the ages of five or six will already have chosen "their basic sexual orientation" and experiences during their adolescent development only serve to "affirm or reject" their earlier sexual preferences.

When questioned by a school board lawyer, Dr. Friedman said "strong, domineering women teachers" pose a greater threat to the sexual adjustment of young, impressionable boys. He explained that young boys, chafing under the role of a stern woman, could conceivably turn to other males for affection, having acquired a fear or dislike for all females.

Dr. John Money, of Johns Hopkins University, who is a specialist in the field of gender identity development, was asked whether Joe's presence in the earth science classroom (where human sexuality is not appropriately discussed by any teacher) would influence students' sexual orientation. Dr. Money responded:

... it is well-nigh universal for all children of eighth-grade age level to know a good deal about human sexuality, including homosexuality. They get this from television, from reading, from the general media ... [and] from people of their own age group. One person in the classroom is not, by any means, the sole source of influence. ... At this age, children are very important influences on each other, the so-called influence of the peer group.

I have talked with young people who knew that a teacher in their junior high school was, ostensibly, homosexual, and I found out there that a very important factor can be that the boys monitor one another, so to speak, away from homosexuality, which is a taboo for them, since they are all, the majority of them, striving toward heterosexuality.

For example, I heard from one boy representing and talking about his school—and he was at that stage—that although they were not sure that a certain teacher was a homosexual, it was part of the gossip, and any time they saw a member of their group with any kind of behavior or habit or mannerism, in any way, shape, or form, resembling what that teacher would do, they brought it to the attention of the person showing it, with possibly a little badgering, possibly a little bantering, and sort of made sure that he got rid of it; so, they were actually monitoring themselves as a group very strongly toward heterosexuality.

Now, one can think of the example of the shy and extremely inhibited boy who has a very strong homosexual or bisexual component to his personality who doesn't do very well with fitting in with his age mates and because of his tendency is rather ostracized by them. This kind of boy, by having a knowledge of a teacher's homosexuality, who is not some type of stereotypic freak, a dangerous person, but is a regular human being who seems to be able to behave and conduct himself in a regular human kind of way, this kind of boy may find some help in his own tremendous anxieties and dilemmas, because a boy who has to discover himself bisexually or homosexually usually is pretty much affected by anxiety, since he knows that it is not the way things were planned for him, and he really needs someone to be able to talk to, someone to be able to disclose his inner anxieties to.

Ideally, he should be able to go to his parents and, traditionally, he is supposed to have been able to go to his doctor or his pastor or priest, but often his anxieties are so great that they prevent him from talking to anybody.

So, with the example of someone who doesn't seem to be a complete monster, it may give him a sense of freedom that he can, in fact, disclose the dilemma that he is struggling with by going to his parents or his counselor at school or the preacher at church or the synagogue or the local physician, and if he does that, then he has the greatest possible chance of having either his anxieties alleviated or, in some cases, to strengthen the heterosexual component of his personality so that he may, in fact, be able to veer more in the heterosexual rather than in the homosexual direction, especially if that is really the way he would prefer things to be.

Because so much misunderstanding surrounds our notions of how an adult role model's sexuality may or may not affect young people, it will probably be a long time before parents and school boards cease to fear that homosexual teachers will "recruit" their children. It has been estimated that between 10 and 20 percent of teachers in any school system are gay, either actively or as celibates. Teaching has always attracted single men and women who don't have many dependents to support, who have few other young people in their lives, and who enjoy a long summer of restful privacy.

Private schools, summer camps, and youth groups of all kinds have always been heavily staffed by gay personnel. (When Nancy asked her twelve-year-old how many gay women work at her summer riding camp, Abby replied simply, if hyperbolically, "Millions.") The fact is that a lot of gay adults work well with youngsters and feel that they have something to offer them; no one understands the pain and panic of growing up better than they do.

As homosexuality comes to be more openly dealt with in the media, and as associations of gay teachers receive more support from unions and from younger people now entering the profession, the situation should improve substantially. Teachers in progressive communities are beginning to come out of the closet and the bandwagon effect is bound to force school officials to reevaluate their positions. And students, together with enlightened parents, can protest the removal of excellent teachers from the classroom on grounds of immorality where none is evident.

In higher education, of course, there is less harassment of gay people. Students at universities and colleges all over the country are forming gay associations that are registered and funded as official campus activities. In 1977 gay students at Virginia Commonwealth University won official recognition in a decision by the U.S. Fourth Circuit Court of Appeals. The court decided that denial of recognition to any group by a state agency constituted a denial of the group's constitutional rights under the First Amendment.

Older gays have been relatively inactive on university campuses, perhaps because, contrary to popular assumption, professors can be almost as conservative as university administrators. The board of trustees, which has the last word on policy, is usually the most conservative of all, and no one wants to offend the wealthy alumnus whose financial support is threatened by radical stirrings on campus. One University of Delaware professor was fired because he defended the activities of a gay student group. A district court judge ordered him reinstated, with back pay and fifteen thousand dollars in damages, and forbade discrimination against him in the future. But the alarm set up by the university president's defamation of his character created such a disagreeable climate for this professor that he accepted an appointment elsewhere for the following academic year.

To get firsthand information about gays in the health professions, we talked with Dr. Walter Y. in a large eastern city. He told us about how an established physician comes out of the closet. For him it was unusually easy, because he worked for the public health administration of a state whose progressive governor had issued a directive prohibiting discrimination on the basis of sexual orientation in the hiring of state employees.

Until his late forties, Dr. Y. lived a double life—privately with his lover of twenty years, and publicly as a distinguished physician. Many of his oldest friends didn't even know he had a lover until he decided to end the charade, a move he considered primarily political, enabling him to work more effectively for the improvement of gay health care services.

Dr. Y. feels strongly that many gay people do not get adequate care because they are not encouraged to be honest about their medical histories and sexual practices. They know that doctors discriminate. For example, an Oregon study showed that 80 percent of doctors would prefer not to take a gay patient. Concealment of relevant data can affect diagnoses and recommendations for disease prevention, and as a consequence social diseases can often reach epidemic proportions in gay communities. A climate of mutual mistrust between doctor and patient often discourages homosexuals from following the advice they do receive. This is also true in the field of mental health, where community health services personnel are often poorly informed about variations in sexual orientation and may therefore further confuse their already troubled clients. Furthermore, group treatment programs in drug abuse, alcoholism, as well as other types of therapy frequently exclude gay patients through a misguided fear that they will disrupt the group interaction. Dr. Y. knew that he was in a position to improve this type of situation because of his status in the field of public health, so in 1972 he made the decision to come out officially.

We asked him about the problems an openly gay physician might face. Dr. Y. told us that hospitals and medical teams tend to be very conservative; few organizations dare to take on an openly gay associate unless he or she has some specialized talent that is unavailable otherwise. Most M.D.s are in private practice, to be sure, but the situation is not totally different there because the status of a private practitioner is frequently determined by his or her colleagues. It is they who refer patients and determine rank in the hospital hierarchy.

The job situation is particularly difficult for gay nurses, Dr. Y. told us, because they are almost always employed by a hospital, nursing home, or other medical institution. Many nurses, both men and women, are gay, but Dr. Y. knows of no hospital where an effort is made to deal with that fact in a rational way. Supervisors are often older, conservative women who wield their authority with a heavy hand, and in Dr. Y.'s opinion, repressed sexual energy creates a real personality problem for many of them. We ourselves know of cases where nurses suspected of having a homosexual relationship were harassed by a supervisor on the job and ultimately fired for some other, specious, reason.

Many opportunities still exist for the openly gay physician. A family practitioner, for example, can have less contact with organized medicine and referrals are less important. Dr. Brian T. started to practice internal medicine in the District of Columbia at the age of thirty-two. There is no sign on his door stating his sexual orientation, nor does he keep copies of *Playgirl* in his waiting room, but about half of his patients are homosexuals. Brian works part-time at the Gay Men's V.D. Clinic. His nongay patients come to him largely through colleagues with whom he worked as a resident in infectious diseases at a Veterans Administration hospital. A patient comes to a hospital emergency room, for instance, and turns out to have no private physician, so Brian gets a referral if follow-up treatment by an internist is needed.

Working under an established practitioner does not appeal to him. He says that he couldn't stand having to play it straight, pretending to be interested in girls. He plans no academic, high-prestige career where being openly gay would mean a constant battle for advancement. Brian's strongly religious, ethnically oriented family need never find out about his homosexuality. There will be career compromises, but they will be based on his own decisions as to what is best for him personally and professionally. He will be a competent physician, in a limited field, at peace with his prospects for the future.

In the course of our conversation with Brian we found out about the Gay Medical Students' Association, an officially recognized subdivision of the American Medical Students' Association. Jaimie S., a third-year student at a prominent eastern medical school, was one of its founders. When we talked to him, there was a membership of about fifty students from medical schools all over the country.

Jaimie was bisexual in high school but lived with a woman for three years while at college in California. He finally came to accept his homosexual preference during graduate school at Stanford and decided that the bisexual life he might have preferred presented too many social and personal problems. At twenty-one, he told his parents about it. Jaimie's father expressed some guilt about not having spent more time with the four children, of whom Jaimie is the eldest. Jaimie told him that he was happy and comfortable: "If you had any part in it, thank you!"

We asked this outgoing young man whether he thought that being gay would affect his career. He told us that he lives exactly as he chooses. He and his lover own a home in a once-elegant section of the inner city, now being restored, and they move socially together as a couple. At medical school parties they dance together if they feel like it. Jaimie is 100 percent out of the closet, though he does not consider himself an activist and feels no need to discuss the issue with casual acquaintances "unless it comes up." He was not fully committed to gay life when he applied to medical school but feels that this would have made no difference "unless an issue was made of it." He says that he personally knows about twenty other gay medical students, four or five of whom are out to the same extent he is. Ideally, a group practice lies ahead. In an urban area this should be no problem; Jamie has no intention of trying to break into small-town society. Public health work also interests him, and he would like the opportunity to do some teaching on a part-time basis. If he ever decides to set up a private practice, he is confident of getting support and approval from nongay friends because he places great value on integrating his life with that of the majority, or heterosexual, community. And when he takes his medical boards and applies for a license, Jaimie expects his professors' support. He believes that he can stand on his own merits. Talking with him, we never doubted it for a minute.

The motives behind the creation of a Gay Nurses Alliance, a Task Force on Homosexuality and the Gay Community of the National Conference of Social Welfare, and an Association of Gay Psychologists have been nearly identical. Gay professionals in these fields know that the problems of homosexual patients and clients are poorly understood and in many cases insensitively handled. Members of these professions have been slow to face the fact that gay nurses, gay social workers, and gay psychologists even exist. It is even more threatening to face the possibility that homosexual professionals are particularly well qualified to help the gay mother on welfare, the gay drug addict, the gay foster child. The homophile organizations mentioned above are dedicated to the correction of this inequity in services. The Association of Gay Psychologists has as one of its objectives the establishment of gay community service centers, gay counseling centers, and gay studies programs. A start is being made, but there is much more to be done. The Task Force on Homosexuality and the Gay Community has presented programs at meetings of the National Conference on Social Welfare on such topics as "Gay Parents and Gay Children," dealing with foster care. Over one thousand nurses attended a Gay Nurses Alliance program entitled "Gay People/Straight Health Care" at an American Nurses Association Convention.

The first work-based organization in the gay movement was the American Library Association Task Force on Gay Liberation. Begun in 1970 and sponsored by ALA's social-activism wing, the task force has worked actively to maintain and circulate an up-to-date bibliography of gay literature for use in library book selection. The bibliography emphasizes nonfiction materials, including articles, pamphlets, periodicals, and audiovisual aids, but it also includes fiction, plays, and biography. Bookstores, counseling services, religious organizations, and libraries of all kinds use it to keep abreast of recent publications in which homosexuality and gay life are treated fairly and objectively rather than as an illness or criminal condition.

Librarianship is a popular field among gays. The men find that they can advance rapidly in a field that has been dominated by women for so long, and single women are free to serve the evening and weekend hours that cause such problems for the working homemaker. Furthermore, gay librarians are recognized and accepted to a degree that is unusual in most professions. There has been long-standing support for gays within the professional hierarchy; in 1977 the elected policy-making ALA Council passed a strong gay rights resolution: "Council reaffirms its support for equal employment opportunity for gay librarians and library workers."

The resolution also affirms that to "combat the current campaign against full human rights for gay American citizens, Council recommends that libraries reaffirm their obligation under the Library Bill of Rights to disseminate information representing all points of view on this controversial subject."

In law, as in many other fields, what you know is not necessarily the only significant factor in career success. Whom you know and how well you know them can be an equally important factor. Clients may take potential business elsewhere if one member of a firm is known to be gay. Judges and juries who bear prejudice against homosexuals can be adversely influenced against a plaintiff or defendant who is represented by a gay lawyer.

We know one attorney in a "progressive" southern city, for example, who handles family and divorce cases. His partners know he's gay, but the office staff is officially in the dark, and only clients who know him personally are aware of his sexual preferences. He lobbies for gay rights, but as an American Civil Liberties Union member, not as a gay activist.

Another young man, Carl Z., has just passed his Maryland bar examination after achieving magna cum laude status in law school, where he was the only button-wearing activist in his class. However, Carl allowed friends to persuade him not to antagonize his exam board by raising the issue at the time of the exam. He feels that he compromised his integrity somewhat by making that decision, but he is certainly going to be able to fight the system more effectively from within it than he could have had the bar association refused to admit him.

There is no guarantee, of course, that Carl would have been refused admittance in any case. In 1973 the New York Court of Appeals ordered that a self-proclaimed homosexual be admitted to the bar, and since then gay identity per se has not been cause for exclusion, although few lawyers want to precipitate lengthy, expensive litigation even when it means opening their career to gays. A list of the cities having professional associations of gay lawyers gives a good idea of where safety lies—they are Los Angeles, San Francisco (2), Morristown, New Jersey (2), Chicago (2, including a Gay Law Students Association), and New York. Such organizations are rapidly growing in membership and in number, and they have increasing political clout. For example, George Raya of San Francisco, who helped found the University of California Gay Law Students Association, was one of a gay citizens' delegation meeting with former presidential aide Margaret Costanza in 1977 to present problems faced by gay Americans. He is working with officials from the Department of Health, Education and Welfare on improving research and social services to aged persons and community groups having homosexual orientation.

The growing number of gay political figures who have chosen to emerge from their closets is another promising sign. Elaine Noble, for example, won her seat in the Massachusetts legislature as an avowed gay. She was one of three lesbians named to President Carter's 51.3% Committee on the status of women, and her excellent reputation as an intelligent and responsive legislator has earned her nationwide recognition, as well as a second term in office. Alan

Spear, a gay history professor, has served several terms in the Minnesota state legislature. And on the municipal level, Kathy Kozechenko made history with her election to the Ann Arbor, Michigan, city council in 1974, and Jim Yeadon became Madison, Wisconsin's, first openly gay alderperson in 1977 by gaining 58 percent of the vote.

On Capitol Hill, gay activist Gary Aldridge works as an aide to Senator Alan Cranston. Any aide's job is politically sensitive, and there has been some criticism from the grass roots, but Gary tells us that the senator probably gets more support than opposition for his liberal position. He himself is working with a dozen or so other aides to create a gay caucus on the Hill. Their hope is to create a more positive climate of opinion so that at least some of the hundreds of closeted congressional staff members will feel free to follow his example.

Gary, like so many other gay professionals, feels strongly that "successful role models must come out in order to change people's perceptions of the average gay person." He knows from processing the letters from his home state that "people are convinced that there are no gay teachers, policemen, firemen. Legislators fear to open the floodgates to people they've never encountered before" by supporting equal employment legislation. Gary says, "I'm glad I did it. My energy is better spent in other ways—I got tired of hiding behind trees when TV cameras photographed a gay event. I have a better-integrated life now, a better personality. I can do better work since I'm happier and more confident."

Gay voting power is still a virtually untapped resource, largely because of lack of any cohesive leadership. Its impact is usually most significant in local, urban elections, because gays, like any minority, tend to group in neighborhoods. Where an organized gay community does exist, politicians are quite aware of its possibilities. For example, in 1970, gay voting power tipped the balance in a New York City Council election. No Democrat had been elected from the wealthy (Upper East Side) 66th District for fifty-six years, but a massive effort by politically oriented gay leaders put Democrat Antonio Olivieri over the top by five hundred votes, in recognition of his support for the fledgling gay rights movement.

More recently, Ed Koch of New York, who introduced the 1977 Gay Civil Rights Bill when he was in Congress, received strong support from gay New Yorkers in his successful race for mayor. On the West Coast, Mayor Wes Uhlman of Seattle received badly needed support from that city's influential, business-oriented Dorian Group and the homophile community at large because of his positive stand on gay rights.

Even some of our unions, often thought to be bastions of redneck conservatism, are beginning to catch on. Local 16 of the National Association of Broadcast Employees and Technicians got strike support from the New York Gay Activist Alliance in return for NABET endorsement of a 1977 GAA rally at the United Nations. In San Francisco, teamster union locals have worked with gay rights groups. If this sounds incongruous, interviews reveal that many homosexual couples work as long-haul truckers because they enjoy the privacy and independence afforded by the job.

A career in federal government service offers good job security for gay people, with certain exceptions. In the military it is still virtually impossible to survive out of the closet, though regulations are inconsistently enforced and some changes appear to be on the way. The various security agencies (CIA, FBI, National Security Administration) also mistrust homosexuals on account of the old blackmail myth that says gays can't be trusted with secrets because they are unstable and have seamy private lives to protect. A career in most departments that deal with foreign relations presents the same problem though the State Department has agreed to abide by the District of Columbia's antidiscrimination ordinance. Gays who work for the State Department are safe, but only if their paychecks are issued in the District of Columbia itself.

However, in any agency whose hiring is governed by Civil Service regulations (that of the above-named agencies is not), gays can now officially come out of the closet. This is a fairly recent, highly encouraging development in the history of gay civil rights. A series of court challenges encouraged the Civil Service Commission to amend its official hiring policies in 1975; homosexuals can now be terminated only in cases where there is evidence that their sexual practices affect job fitness. Terminations based on unsubstantiated conclusions about possible embarrassment to the federal service are no longer grounds for discrimination in hiring or promotions. Agencies not controlled by Civil Service policies are gradually following suit, one by one. In 1977, for example, the Job Corps and the Agency for International Development office reversed their policies of rejecting gay applicants.

This doesn't mean that everyone who works for the government has felt free to jump out of the closet at once; many personal factors are involved. If you come out at work and your boss doesn't happen to like gay people— well, we asked Cheryl, a black woman quoted in the previous chapter, to comment on that:

The only place I'm real uptight about being gay is at work. I've been working for the post office for three years, and somehow I just don't want them to know. I don't know what would happen, but it just doesn't seem like a real good idea. My supervisor, for one thing, he flirts all the time; nothing real bad, just little looks and laughs with the girls, and if you get on his wrong side he can really screw you. He couldn't fire me unless he had proof I was a bad worker, because the union is pretty strong, but he can change your shift around, or put you in the dirtiest job with the oldest broken-down machines and just make you miserable. If you treat him right you get treated all right, but if I was to say, "Fuck off, Harvey," he'd have my ass in the back room with no breaks forever. He would not like me being gay; it would irk him, so I just keep to myself.

Jay Armstrong works for the post office, too. He is thirty-seven years old, tall, good-looking, with a pleasant but firmly assertive manner. Jay works actively with his local gay community and talks comfortably over the counter with us when we come in to mail packages. But speaking of a younger coworker, a carrier, he says, "I know he's not out yet. He's got that scared look about him all the time." That's the crux of the matter, right there. People *are* scared—that their parents might find out, that coworkers will sneer at them or turn their backs, or that someone will get drunk and decide to beat them up some night. But for someone who does want to come all the way out, the Civil Service is a good bet.

Air force Sergeant Leonard Matlovich found that being a closet gay in the military was an uneasy and unhappy role to maintain. At thirty-two he had twelve years of service, including three tours in Vietnam, and had won a Bronze Star and a Purple Heart. Although he had known from the age of twelve that men attracted him, Matlovich says that until he was thirty he literally thought he was the only such person in the world. He finally found out otherwise in a Florida gay bar and then wrestled with the problem for two years afterward. "I was teaching a course in human relations," he told us, "telling other soldiers to get involved, to act on their convictions. I had to do it myself. My conscience was beginning to eat me alive."

Sgt. Matlovich was discharged posthaste, after declaring his homosexuality in a letter to a superior officer. He knew then that had he chosen to be discreet, to meet men off base as others do, he could have expected a trouble-free military career. When we asked him to compare the pressure on gays in the various services, he told us that the navy is probably most tolerant because of its long-standing traditions: young boys used to be kept on board for sex, cabin boys for the captain and "powder monkeys" for the crew. The air force seems to be particularly homophobic, since regulations permit discharge of anyone who even displays suspicious habits. One friend of his was discharged for "homosexual tendencies and habitual association with Leonard Matlovich."

But increasing leniency is apparent now at all levels in every branch of the service. Supervisors tell their men to ignore the regulations, but to exercise reasonable precaution. Homosexuals of all ranks serve honorably for a lifetime, keeping their sex lives strictly separate from their military duties, just as any responsible soldier is expected to do. Matlovich even knows one general who keeps a male lover at his Georgetown mansion.

A certain amount of pressure is now being put on the military because of possible unconstitutional restrictions on sexual behavior. Matlovich himself is suing the air force and will take his case to the Supreme Court if necessary. Northern California's U.S. District Court of Appeals has ruled that "the Navy's policy of discharging homosexuals without considering all relevant factors pertaining to their fitness to serve . . . free of any policy of mandatory exclusion . . . violates the due process clause of the Fifth Amendment." An army veteran, Charles Brydon of Seattle, has met with members of the Carter administration and Defense Department officials to request immediate upgrading of the more than seventy-five thousand military discharges since World War II.

The proportion of naturally bisexual and homosexual men in the various services is probably about comparable to that in American society as a whole. Under conditions of stress and in combat-type posts where women are scarce, homosexual behavior is bound to arise just because people are going to turn somewhere for emotional and sexual release. This, of course, is an inevitable if temporary phenomenon, quickly "forgotten" when normal life resumes. But among women in the armed forces, just as in women's athletics, the numbers are evidently higher. Lesbians choose to serve because they know they will meet people like themselves and because they don't need men in their lives. Most of the women we know who have been in the services tell us that they never knew anyone who got into trouble, although there is a good deal of pressure evident. They mainly try to get off post to make love, though one woman described sex "in the kitchens, under the beds," anywhere to get some privacy.

The best bet is to obey the "no sex on duty" regulation and conduct oneself in a professional manner at all times. National defense, Matlovich reminded us, is no game. And, since entrance forms no longer ask if the applicant is homosexual, there is no need for the issue to arise.

There are certain types of jobs, some fairly new, in which gays have never suffered discrimination. Computer technology, for example, is reported by many gays to be a comfortable field. Once the word gets around, of course, others are encouraged to go into the same work. In a less organization-oriented profession, where what you can do is more important than what connections you may have, there is less pressure to conform, and a greater chance to meet compatible coworkers. A few jobs are actually dominated by gay males—hairdressing and interior decorating for instance. There, one is often expected to be homosexual, a situation that can be embarrassing for nongays in the field. Female-dominated jobs such as secretarial work and nursing also provide a nonthreatening atmosphere for the less aggressive male.

Two other professions come immediately to mind in terms of nonconformity—sports and the arts. Both require natural ability plus an enormous commitment to excellence, but there the similarity ends. Americans love to think that artists are bizarre, and there is a strong tradition which holds that being creative in an esthetic direction is not manly. It is also not feminine, which is one reason why women have been so loath to shoot for the top in art, literature, or music.

The list of famous homosexual painters, poets, sculptors, actors, composers, and dramatists would fill pages: Handel, Proust, Caravaggio, E. M. Forster, Tennessee Williams, Langston Hughes, Somerset Maugham, Montgomery Clift, Oscar Wilde, Gertrude Stein, among many others. Whether being gay also makes you creative, however, is certainly debatable. Some people feel that seeking the freedom to be yourself fosters freedom to express yourself. Others maintain that homosexuals, as social outcasts, have often been unhappy, and the creative outlet acts as a release for energies stifled elsewhere. Whether there is a correlation or not, it is clear that homosexuals have contributed much more than their share to Western culture.

In sports it's a different story; sports heroes are expected to offer their fans a strongly "macho" image. Popular myth has it that an openly homosexual preference would damage that image beyond repair, and so far no major figure now active in sports has cared to risk his or her reputation in that way. We all remember what Dr. Richard Raskind went through when she chose to resume her amateur tennis career as Renee Richards.

When *The Advocate,* a national gay newspaper, attempted to do a survey on homosexuality in sports, reactions were immediate and violent. The Minnesota Twins' public-relations director wrote in response to *The Advocate*'s request for interviews: "The cop-out, immoral lifestyle of the tragic misfits espoused by your publication has no place in organized athletics at any level . . . [and your attempt] to extend your perversion to an area of total manhood is . . . unthinkable." And yet in 1977 *The New York Times* reported that a Gay Athletes Union claims 1,450 members, most of them college-level varsity athletes from six countries.

In 1975 the *Washington Star* ran a series of articles based on interviews with more than sixty coaches, sports officials, athletes, and psychologists. They came to the not very surprising conclusion that there are about as many gay and bisexual men in sports as elsewhere, from the NFL on down, but that the secret is carefully guarded for obvious reasons. Several retired sports figures have suffered the loss of reputations and businesses when it became known that they were gay. To protect themselves, single men make it a point to talk about women a lot, and many bisexuals maintain the front of a wife and kids. One pro football player told reporters that he lies awake some nights wondering if the lover who just left his bed will be the one who betrays him. Another says that during the season he appears at Jaycee luncheons, charity events, and high school banquets in his home city accompanied by women friends. But from January through June he locates elsewhere to visit gay bars and meet new men without fear of losing his off-season business or being kicked off his team. "People don't see a football player as a person," he says bitterly, "they see you as an object. Christ, we're not objects!"

The proportion of gay women in amateur and professional sports is perhaps three or four times as great as in the population as a whole. Their presence conflicts less with popular stereotypes because independence, aggressiveness, and a competitive spirit are highly desirable on the tennis court and golf course, but less so in the kitchen and nursery. In fact, nongay women in sports deeply resent being put down as unfeminine just because they have a natural ability and interest in competitive sports. Many blame lesbian athletes for fostering this unfavorable image. Gay women, who are accustomed to being resented by just about everybody, try to shrug off the slurs and innuendo. One golfer told reporters, "If people won't accept you as people, whether you're straight or gay or a whore or whatever, then I'm just going to go out and play golf!"

A number of closeted gays are painfully aware that by failing to identify themselves publicly they are indirectly perpetuating all the popular myths about homosexuals. If, on the other hand, they were out, they could be serving as the positive role models gay youngsters need for the development of a good self-image. David Kopay, the former Redskins running back, says his conscience compelled him to fight the hypocrisy by volunteering an interview for the *Washington Star*'s homosexuality series. He said he hoped it might help younger people who are going through similar experiences and haven't had anyone to talk to about it.

There have been so many firsts for gay people in the past few years, and the pace accelerates all the time! A gay TV reporter now works for a San Francisco station. His primary responsibility is to provide objective, informed coverage of news events involving the estimated one hundred thousand gay residents of that city. As Randy Shilts points out himself, "Seeing an openly gay person in a responsible position like a newscaster can have a positive effect on young gays trying to come to terms with themselves."

Often it is frustration over a job discrimination incident that induces someone in a traditionally straight profession to stand up and be counted. Guy Hunt, for example, flew Northwest Airlines planes for seven years before he was discharged, ostensibly for refusing to take a physical exam. Since the issue of "instant physicals" had previously sparked controversy between the Airline Pilots Association and airlines' management, the association supported his charge that the real reason was his gay orientation. A labor-management arbitration board has heard the case, but as we go to press we have not heard the result. Hunt was fired in Minneapolis, which has a gay civil rights ordinance, so a complaint was also filed with the city's Human Rights

Commission. As an outgrowth of the dismissal, Hunt and seven other pilots formed a Gay Airline Pilots' Association.

Having it known that individual gays are willing to battle job discrimination is useful in many ways. No corporation or industry wants to create martyrs—it's bad for business. And management is often caught off guard when a discharged employee refuses to crawl away in defeat and shame. As Washington, D.C., gay rights leader Frank Kameny points out, "They don't expect you to fight back." And now and then some courageous individual decides that though his job may be expendable, his pride is not.

Bob M., a nine-year employee of a gas and electric company, describes himself as a "rough-and-tumble-type person." He is very masculine looking, with a deep voice and open manner. He is also an active participant in gay community events but does not believe in allowing his private life to infringe upon his performance on the job.

Bob went to work one day only to be told that he had been "misplaced in his job category," which was installing and repairing major appliances. He went home with his severance pay, but not for long. For five months he hounded two company vice-presidents with the threat of a Federal Equal Opportunities Commission action, until they got so tired of avoiding him that they hired him back. As it turned out, the gas company had already been in trouble over affirmative action orders involving women and blacks.

Bob is in an office job now, at a lower pay rate, so that no customer who might have seen him at a gay rights rally on television can be offended by having him turn up at her house to install a stove. But his job benefits have been restored, and his coworkers are keeping their faggot and ethnic jokes to themselves. As he says, "They accept me for what I am and everybody gets on very nicely. They've got the word—don't back me into a corner because I'll come out fighting." At the mixed league where he bowls, Bob wears his gay rights T-shirts and there is no problem. He has

already served one term as league president. "They don't
care if I'm gay, as long as I can bowl."

Much of this progress toward attainment of equal employment opportunity for gay people has come by way of
federal court decisions. State legislatures, though, have been
slow to generate change. As of this writing, no state has
expanded its civil rights code to include homosexuals except Pennsylvania, which guarantees equality in state employment only. About forty local jurisdictions have enacted
nondiscrimination legislation. The District of Columbia's
Title 34 is the strongest, affording protection in housing,
employment, and public accommodations. Other cities having progressive legislation in these areas include East Lans-
ing, Detroit, and Ann Arbor in Michigan; Berkeley, Palo
Alto, and San Jose in California; Marshall in Minnesota; Portland and Seattle in the Pacific Northwest; Ur-
bana and Bloomington in Indiana; Tucson, Arizona; and
Toronto, Ontario. Recently, however, several cities have re-
scinded these laws, including St. Paul, Wichita, and Eugene.
Several large and small cities prohibit discrimination in
city employment. These include New York; San Francisco;
Atlanta; Los Angeles; Boston; Chapel Hill, North Carolina;
Ithaca, New York; Ottawa, Ontario; Amherst, Massachusetts; and Pullman, Washington. Some counties, too, offer
civil rights to gay people: Howard in Maryland, Hennepin
in Minnesota, and Santa Cruz in California.
It is, in fact, illegal to be a sexually active gay male in
more than half of our United States. Existing laws against
sodomy, which is commonly defined as any unnatural sex
act, especially anal intercourse, are virtually never enforced
against heterosexual couples in our time. They are, however,
frequently used to prosecute gay men. Their existence encourages popularly held beliefs about the perversion attributed to all gays and acts as a substantial deterrent to the
passage of progressive civil rights legislation. As of this

writing, nineteen states have repealed their sodomy laws, which formerly appeared in every state code. But since the Supreme Court recently refused to hear a case challenging the constitutionality of such a law in Virginia, it will no doubt be a long time before states with strongly religious or conservative traditions will give up their right to dictate sexual morality.

The states that repealed sodomy legislation before this book was written are California, Colorado, Connecticut, Delaware, Hawaii, Illinois, Indiana, Iowa, Maine, Nebraska, New Hampshire, New Mexico, North Dakota, Ohio, Oregon, South Dakota, Washington, West Virginia, and Wyoming.

Most of these acts were repealed during the 1970s; indeed, the 1970s brought enormous progress in equality of opportunity for gay people, and the promise of more to come. On the national political scene a civil rights bill for gays gained support steadily, with thirty-nine cosponsors in the 1977 House of Representatives. President Carter also indicated concern for the rights of his gay constituents. On one occasion he said, "I oppose discrimination on the basis of sexual orientation. As president I can assure you that all policies of the federal government will reflect this commitment." Administration representatives were encouraged to cooperate with gay rights organizations, principally the New York–based National Gay Task Force. In Washington, members of the National Gay Rights Lobby work on Capitol Hill and at various government agencies to educate bureaucrats and members of Congress as to the unmet needs of this twenty-million-member, largely invisible constituency.

For example, pressure is being put on the Federal Communications Commission to add gays to the list of sensitive minority and special-interest groups who must be consulted as part of the procedure to renew radio and TV station licenses. The Immigration and Naturalization Service has worked with gay people to reevaluate their regulations governing entry visas for known homosexuals. Responding to National Gay Task Force efforts, the Internal Revenue Service has reversed its policy of refusing tax-exempt status to gay groups. And the Department of Housing and Urban Development is considering the development of guidelines for implementation of fair housing codes on behalf of gay homeowners and tenants.

In the business world, over one hundred major companies and many smaller ones went on record by the end of 1978 with policies of nondiscrimination in hiring and promotions. These include AT&T, IBM, Bank of America, Proctor and Gamble, Avon Products, McDonalds, Honeywell, American and Eastern airlines, CBS, ABC, and Citicorp. Statements by these companies indicate that they do not consider sexual preference relevant to job competence and often add that their personnel departments have been instructed not to inquire into the private lives of employees.

In many cities gay people and their supporters are beginning to realize that gay buying power can carry considerable political and social weight. Dollars speak loudly, and gays control many dollars indeed. For example, a 1977 issue of *New York* magazine reported the results of a survey conducted by *Blueboy,* which is a magazine for gay men. The *Blueboy* reader is between twenty-five and forty years old and earns between fifteen and twenty-five thousand dollars a year. He has a college degree and some graduate education, carries several major credit cards, owns an American car, and takes two to three vacations annually. He smokes, he buys brand-name liquor; he spends five hundred to a thousand dollars a year on clothes, and the same amount on TV, hi-fi, and camera equipment. Surveys indicate that over eight hundred thousand men read *Blueboy* on a regular basis.

Yet an influential gay person is much less willing to emerge from the closet than a young rebel with little of value to lose by coming out publicly. For example, no prominent homosexual from Wall Street, Madison Avenue, or New York's Seventh Avenue garment district has ever admitted to gay identity, though estimates indicate that gay New Yorkers control up to twenty *billion* dollars.

But one way that lesbians and gay men have found to make their presence felt in a relatively nonthreatening way is through the formation of gay business and professional associations. These groups enlist the support of businesses and nongay professional people who wish to encourage gay customers and who are willing to declare themselves un-biased in the hiring and promotion of employees. Seattle's Dorian Group serves as a model for this type of organiza-tion.

Charles Brydon, ex-president of the Dorian Group and northwest manager of the AFIA Worldwide Insurance Company, told us that three years after the group was formed, its mailing list had over twelve hundred names. Prominent citizens from throughout the state of Washington address members at monthly luncheon meetings. Civil rights for all people are actively promoted by the group's political wing, and a continuing educational program sends speakers to talk with any group desiring to become better informed about homosexuality or the gay community. Associations of this type serve to integrate gay and nongay grcups and individuals who share a common interest in ending job discrimination. They also encourage closeted gay people to promote their own rights and interests in a supportive atmosphere where it may be possible to ease gradually out of the closet.

And so, it may be difficult, there may be obstacles, but in general gays can pick their profession and, more and more frequently, be granted the right to live their private lives as they wish.

6

Gay Couples

One of the principal concerns felt by every loving parent is that his or her child find happiness in marriage. For parents who know that a child is gay, this hope may seem at first to be a tragic farce. The possibility that a gay relationship can provide the same rich rewards offered by traditional marriage seems farfetched, especially for those who have heard only myths or secondhand reports about gay life. Loneliness and a string of foundering romances seem to lie ahead, to be followed by years of miserable, solitary old age.

We as parents feel particularly glad to have good news from this front, because we share the same concern—we want our son and daughter to experience the emotional benefits of a firm, mature commitment to that one person whose love will mean more than anything in the world. And it does happen. Gay men and women fall in love and live happily, just as traditional couples do. Someone comes along who can meet all the deeply felt needs: for companionship, for sharing, for support, for that extra measure of understanding and warmth that makes Johnny or Jane feel like the most important and the luckiest person in the world. Many such relationships last a lifetime; others serve their purpose for a while but fail to stand the test of time, so that after a year, or five years, or longer, the two grow apart and decide to break it off.

Most gay people with whom we talk seem to feel that being involved in a long-term, stable relationship offers their greatest chance for personal fulfillment. Those who now have, or who once had, that experience consider it enriching; parents who are well acquainted with their child's life-style often come to understand that their child benefits from sharing life with another person and sanction the relationship by accepting the lover as they would a legal spouse.

We interviewed several young couples, and some not so young, to ask them about their values in terms of commitment, fidelity, and goals for the future. We also asked what personal needs were met by the relationship, and why they feel that loyalty to one person is a more rewarding way of life than simply dating a variety of friends.

One recurrent point made in our interviews was the necessity for the personal stability that derives from simply having someone to come home to at night. For younger people it is especially important; possessed of boundless energy and few financial responsibilities, finding the ties of family life restrictive, there is a real temptation to go out every night, to try anything and everything, to "live it up." Carole, for instance, who is now twenty and has been with Bobbie for over a year, pointed this out at once:

She got me out of a lot of bad things I was into. My father had just died, my mother is an invalid, my sister has her own family. I was working on The Block [a local honky-tonk and red-light district], spending every afternoon in the bar. There didn't seem to be anyplace else to go where I could be around people. I didn't want to be alone.

My mother was really glad when I moved in here. She could see that it was having a good effect on me. She likes Bobbie a lot; once she even introduced her in church as her adopted daughter.

Bobbie's family was slower to come around. Her aunt, who raised Bobbie from the age of thirteen, was mistrustful of Carole at first. In recent months, however, their deep love has reassured her. Bobbie told us: "At first it was, 'You care more about Carole than you do about me!' but by the time Christmas came around she was asking, 'When are you and Carole coming over? Do you want separate gifts or something for the house?' "

Tod, twenty-five, has been going to law school in a city several hundred miles from his hometown. His parents often make derogatory comments about gays, and so far he has been able to avoid telling them that Gary, his landlord, is also his lover. Unfortunately, or perhaps fortunately for their peace of mind, his parents have no way of knowing what a difference that relationship has made in his life.

In college I dated girls and even lived with a woman for a while, but I always found men easier to be with and when I moved away from home I decided that I was basically gay. Because I wanted to meet other gay men, I started going to the bars and pretty soon it was every night. Superficially I liked the life; I was into poppers, a lot of drinking, I chain-smoked and watched endless TV. On weekends it was five o'clock until midnight in the bars. I never really liked that person (myself) but I was in a rut.

When he first met Gary, a high school art teacher, it was "love at first sight." ("He quit smoking in two weeks," Gary added. "That ought to tell you something about the nature of our relationship!") Tod continued:

From the very first I knew I wanted a long-term commitment to him, but of course you don't make that kind of promise at the beginning. We sort of set it up as a one-year probation period, like an engagement or trial marriage. During that time we've tried to renew our commitment every day, to counteract the distractions of our jobs and all the other activities we get involved in. Now the year is almost up and we're pretty much to the point of planning major investments for the future.

Right now they live in the home that Gary bought for himself at the conclusion of a six-year marriage, and they describe their life-style as that of a "traditional couple." We asked them about that, and Gary said:

It's important to us to have a nice home that affords comfort, and it's important to have something to do there. You have to make a nest and live in it. It's good to just be able to stay home on a Saturday night and watch TV, for example, or work on a project around the house, or study, as Tod has been doing for his bar exam. Having to maintain a frenetic social life isn't healthy.

When we asked them how they feel about themselves now, after a year together, Gary told us:

Being one of a couple, you're affirmed. It has to affirm your own existence. For myself, I'm a loner in many respects. I can be perfectly contented staying home alone, planning an art project, reading, studying, what have you. But being with Tod, I see myself as a more important, bigger person. Being a couple, you know you're someone in the other person's eyes. And relating to other people, you build up a force. There are two of you, solid against the world.

Tod added:

I'm proud of Gary. It makes me feel good to be seen with him, to have people know we belong together. So what if we're gay—we're not freaks! With salespeople, for instance, when we shop for furniture or something, I think it's important to let them know that we're making a joint decision about purchases, that we're a couple. Because I love and admire him so much I feel as though I want to shout it to the world.

Gary feels that belonging to somebody adds to a person's self-esteem; we asked Tim, a writer in his late twenties, to comment. Tim has had a few heterosexual love affairs and two previous homosexual liaisons, but George, a hospital administrator, is the person with whom he now hopes to spend the rest of his life. He told us:

Look at it this way. Even single people get plants and animals to take care of. People feel more worthy if someone depends on them. You get feedback on your effectiveness as a human being when you're acting as a positive influence on someone's life. Having a responsibility, making a contribution to another person, gives you a role. Sometimes you have to change your idea of yourself to fit the other person's needs, but that's a growing experience.

For example, it's important to me to be able to take care of myself financially and emotionally, and I wasn't too happy at first about letting myself depend on George. He likes to do housework and cooking, for example, and in that sense he really takes care of me. I've learned that George needs to feel that I need him, and I'm learning to accept that.

The question of who assumes which role in a relationship is one that most of the young people we know do not consider. Any division of labor in the home occurs naturally, as a matter of individual temperament and personal preference. Among older gays, however, and even now in conservative communities where virtually everyone is rigidly closeted, the rule that says one has to be a tough, aggressive "butch" and the other a passive, yielding "femme" can still be considered valid. We asked Pat T., whom we met one evening in a working-class women's bar, what her friends think about this kind of role-playing. Pat is thirty-one. "When I was coming out," she said, "we emulated what we saw at home—one washes the dishes, you know. The newer generation has found out that when women are free you can be what you want, no stereotypes. But me—I'm happy with me being butch. It's not necessary, but when I meet two people I wonder which is butch and which is femme. I'm conditioned, you might say."

Bobbie and Carole, of the newer generation, used to frequent a similar type of bar. Bobbie commented with amusement on the "conditioned" attitudes of the older patrons.

We'd sit at one end of the bar and the older crowd would be down at the other end, watching us and trying to figure out which was which. They called us the "neither-nors," told us we were just mixed-up kids who hadn't learned yet whether we were butch or femme. But that kind of arrangement isn't for us. There are times when I'm more dominant and times when Carole is. When people ask me am I femme, I tell them, "If I wanted a man I'd get a man. I love her *because* she's a woman, like me!"

We also talked with Lynne and Sandy who are in their mid-thirties, well educated, and generally out to family and friends, as well as to professional colleagues. Lynne, a musician, is presently putting Sandy through college. They told us that among their friends it is considered passé for partners to base their relationship on the traditional male-female model. And, they see a connection between freedom to be yourself in society and freedom to express your true nature at home. The habit of secrecy, as Lynne says, breeds guilt, and an internalized negative attitude creates strains that are reflected in one's home life.

Lynne and Sandy try to develop both the "male" and the "female" sides of their nature, but they say that practical problems sometimes arise.

With two men or two women, each brings a particular skill, but there may be voids. Neither one may know how to sew, or to fix a roof. We try to do everything around the house ourselves, but sometimes we feel paralyzed when something goes wrong. The myth of "I don't know how to do this" is hard to overcome. We need each other's support, and we need a book.

It's exciting to learn that you're competent. We just built a storage shed and it's sturdy. You can jump up and down on the roof. Our neighbors don't always know what to make of us but the husbands sometimes offer to help when we're stuck.

You can see they admire our independence, even though they wouldn't want their wives to try it.

Lots of funny things can come up when two women live together and share different roles. One friend of ours got a bottle of Shalimar, a box of black lace panties, and a Skilsaw under the Christmas tree. But why not be able to take care of yourself and smell good at the same time?

Liberation from heterosexually based role models, however, does not imply that these couples consider a healthy partnership to be a sexual free-for-all. Many young people are surprisingly idealistic, showing a deep respect for their own sexuality and that of others. They believe that sex should serve the relationship, not the other way around. The issue of fidelity between couples is often discussed, but the strongest arguments are usually in its favor, if only for practical reasons. Most gay people have had ample opportunity to observe, or experience, the difficulty of trying to keep one's emotional loyalties intact when one's sexual loyalties are divided.

One recent session at the Coalition of Gay Sisters in Columbia, Maryland, was devoted to a discussion of monogamy and fidelity in relationships between women. The consensus seemed to be, "Playing around may work for some couples, but personally, I couldn't handle it." One woman said:

I'm not sure which way it works. Maybe when you're young you're not mature enough to fight the jealousy of knowing that there are other people in her life. But maybe it's the other way around—you have to be really mature to build a monogamous relationship and make it work. You have to learn to trust and let the other live her own life. Trying to be everything to each other is stifling. It doesn't let you grow.

Florence, who is sixty-three and blind, gave an illustration from her own life. After the death of her first lover, with whom she had lived for twenty years, she met Jeanne, who is not yet forty and was drawn to her after an unhappy marriage.

Jeanne loves her motorcycle, but you couldn't get me on one of those things! I'm glad she has a friend to go riding with—I like to know she's having a good time. If I asked her to give that up, or if I worried all the time about what else she might be doing, I'd be miserable. And I'd be making her miserable at the same time!

Lynne and Sandy tell us that they try not to worry about it. Sandy said:

Lynne travels a lot in her job with the symphony. I'm not afraid she'd do anything, but if . . . ? We probably could deal with that. For me it would be important to make sure that there were no outstanding unresolved problems between us. If something did turn out to be wrong it could mean we needed to redefine our relationship. Anyhow, we'd try to discuss it rationally.

Maybe it isn't even the sex that's most important. I know I'd be terribly hurt if I thought she would talk to anyone else about the things we talk about together. I was discussing the subject of fidelity with a gay man once and he said, about his lover, "He can do whatever he wants as long as there's no kissing." I guess some men could do that, but I don't know any woman who could relate to a sexual experience without some kind of affection and caring.

Carole and Bobbie, who are younger and socialize with a number of unattached women, take fidelity very seriously. As Bobbie said, "If either of us started seeing another woman I'm sure it would divide us." And Carole added, "I'm very old-fashioned. I believe in monogamy and 'till death do us part.' There's a difference between having sex and making love; having sex is a bed-hopping thing, but making love expresses the emotional connection."

Neither has been tempted to stray during the year they have been together, and they agree that if a rival appeared neither one would give up easily. "I would fight to save the relationship" is the way they put it. "We want to grow old together, and that's something worth putting a lot of effort into."

The value of monogamy in a relationship is not restricted to women. Tim and George both feel that it is "100 percent important," but that if a slip should occur they would talk about it. And Tim added, "If we live together, this is essential." For George, who grew up in a fundamentalist religious community, the emphasis on sex in the context of a primary relationship is basic to his sense of personal dignity. When his marriage dissolved, largely because of sexual incompatibility, and he began to explore gay society, his first impression was that "you have to be faggy and trashy to fit into gay life." George was relieved to find Tim, who was self-respecting and gay at the same time. They feel that their love is based on mutual respect and admiration for each other's values, and that increases the physical attraction between them as well. Each takes a great deal of pride in the social value of his own work, for example, and they admire one another's commitment to a job well done. Love and kindliness are also important values for them. As Tim said, "I saw how wonderful George was with his kids. Seeing your lover involved in a loving, noncompetitive relation with others is important. Each of us values the other as a loving human being. I wasn't about to let someone like that get away."

Unlike many gay couples, for whom the idea of formalizing their union by means of a public ceremony would serve no purpose, Tim and George are planning a marriage celebration. They want their friends, and particularly their families, to witness a taking of vows, and they feel that their commitment will be strengthened thereby. Because they are not members of any religious community, their union will not be sanctioned by any particular institution. But for Bobbie and Carole it was necessary to receive the blessing of a church, and the Holy Union conducted for them at Metropolitan Community Church filled that need. Bobbie says, "Neither of us knew if there was such a thing as a gay wedding, but I suddenly knew (after two and a half weeks together) that if there was, this was who I wanted to marry." Carole added, "I had been lying there wondering about vows. Right then Bobbie asked whether I'd marry her, if there was such a thing. We both got so excited that at two-thirty in the morning there we were on the phone to New Jersey, asking Bobbie's ex-lover if she knew anything about gay weddings."

The ceremony took place nine months ago, in the presence of only two witnesses. "We didn't know whether our families would take it seriously," they said, "and anyway, it was for us, not for a bunch of other people."

We asked the Reverend Stan Harris of Metropolitan Community Church in Baltimore to explain his views on how a formal ceremony of any kind serves to strengthen a couple's chances of remaining together and sustaining fidelity. His answer was that simply making the promise, in an atmosphere of religious solemnity, before witnesses, is an act that fosters maturity and gives meaning to sexual relationships. In his experience, the idea that a perfect relationship means everybody's doing his own thing characterizes the immature person:

Open relationships may sound good in theory but they never seem to end nicely. Infidelity usually chips away at the foundations. The tradition of monogamous marriage was established for good reasons. Moses was a clever man.

You hear some couples say, "If it gets too bad I'll just walk away from it." That probably means they aren't mature enough to carry it off. But even the attempt to do it is a good thing. The second time around, it often works better. You learn something every time you make a serious effort to maintain a stable relationship.

The Reverend Harris told us that in the questionnaire he prepares for Holy Union candidates, the question of "What true thing would you not want her to tell you?" is answered by 99 percent of women with "I wouldn't want to know if she were playing around." Older women have suggested to us that there may be a cultural factor here. Men are raised to resist the idea of being "tied down" to one woman, whereas girls are taught that stability in relationships is a value. If you are a good person, you make a relationship work, even if that means turning down some interesting, attractive person who is making a play for you.

The Reverend Harris, on the other hand, finds that "men complain more than women do about not being able to find anybody to love." They seem less sure initially of their ability to develop a good relationship, and when they do find one they are generally so grateful that they don't want to jeopardize it by risking an outside affair.

Gary agrees. When we asked him to sum up the value that he and Tod place on fidelity he said:

It's more important in gay relationships than in straight ones even. Sexual loyalty is of greater value for gays because of everything in gay life that works against remaining loyal to one person. Relationships among men are so often based on sex; men "turn on" easily and there's a status attached to being able to "score" any time you want to. That isn't limited to gays, of course. It's true in the nongay world as well, and it's easy to slip into that. Sex is so accessible for gay guys that the priority has to be fidelity, in my mind.

It's easier for heterosexual couples to stay together because they are reinforced in so many ways—by in-laws, parents, children of your own. It shows up in the language even. Traditional couples can talk about "my wife," and "my husband." What do you call your lover when you're talking about him? My friend? My roommate? My partner? In our language the word *lover* sounds illicit. Anyhow, it's so much harder for gay couples to make it that we can't afford to take any risks that might threaten our emotional dependence on each other.

Aside from sexual fidelity, what factors do gay couples consider important in building long-term stability? Sharing common goals for the future is certainly important, and we found that many partners consciously plan the mutual or joint investments that will give them something to work toward together. Predictably, being financially secure enough to build their dream house is a major objective.

Carole told us that she has always wanted a home of her own, and that she knew what it would look like long before she met Bobbie.

I was describing it to her one night, just as I imagined it would be, and Bobbie got up and rummaged around in a desk drawer. When she came back she had a set of drawings. They were floor plans for the house she wants to build someday, and it was my dream house exactly. Three bedrooms, all on one floor, with the master bedroom at one end and a combined living-dining area at the other!

These women live on a working-class income. Bobbie manages a filling station which she hopes one day to be able to buy, and Carole has a part-time job in a bakery. For them, a modest home in a middle-income neighborhood is probably a high, though realistic, goal. Both Tod and Gary, on the other hand, hold professional degrees. They enjoy Gary's gracious home and upper-middle-income residential neighborhood, but they think Gary's mother is correct in her prediction that he will make one more major move before finally settling down. Tod is interested in buying a large lot in a country atmosphere, where he could oversee the plans and construction of a home for them to share. In addition, both men are interested in urban redevelopment and they would like to invest in inner-city redevelopment property, to be rented as an additional source of income or held for later sale at a profit.

More pressing than either of these projects, however, is the need they both feel for Gary to get out of the teaching profession. Fear of exposure imposes constraints on their activities that Tod particularly has difficulty accepting. They don't dare go to a movie playing near Gary's school, for example, or to a downtown disco where gays and non-gays mix. Even at the annual city fair, Gary keeps thinking he sees a parent behind every booth. Feeling that this kind of pressure is damaging to their relationship, they plan to begin living on Tod's increasingly lucrative law practice as soon as possible so that Gary can explore other careers. They believe that working toward these relatively ambitious goals will bring increased personal satisfaction and at the same time provide the mutual dependency that makes two people into a functioning unit.

The technique of making joint financial investments seems to have worked well for several older couples we know. Women who have managed to accumulate some capital often find that operating a small business together is a way to cement their relationship while at the same time avoiding the problem of job discrimination against women and gays. And among the male couples whom we know well, Ralph and Dick provide a good example. These wealthy men, both in their late forties, have lived together for over twenty years. They presently own one luxurious condominium in the city and another near a popular beach resort where they host elegant parties for mixed groups of old friends and current business associates. Their interests and tastes differ widely, however, and their considerable wealth permits a degree of independence that most couples cannot afford. Ralph's idea of relaxation is an annual ocean cruise, alone. He also enjoys an occasional evening of dancing and bar-hopping, whereas Dick prefers to spend quiet evenings at home whenever he can escape from job-related social events. Nevertheless, they are devoted to one another and harbor no thoughts of separation. When we asked them, separately, to tell us the secret of their successful partnership each said, "We don't try to do everything together, and we have our investments."

Most couples agree that parental acceptance helps to create stability in a relationship. Ralph feels that the support he received from his socially prominent family many years ago was an important factor in helping him to establish a stress-free relationship with Dick, as well as enabling him to integrate his gay-oriented social life with a mainstream position in society. For younger couples whose parents still play a significant part in their lives, this kind of support is particularly important. Just as in traditional marriage, young gay people have difficulty coping with the divided loyalties that stem from "in-law trouble." Bobbie illustrated this point from her own experience.

At the beginning, before my aunt learned to accept Carole, I was really starting to lose touch with my family and I felt guilty about it. My grandmother is in a nursing home and I wasn't visiting her as often as I wanted to because I hated to drive all the way out there alone. When I went to my aunt's she would criticize Carole, and when I stuck up for her there would be an argument. Then, at home, Carole would get mad at me when I tried to explain why my aunt was acting so hateful to her. It was causing fights there, too.

It's a lot easier for everybody now. Last week my aunt called to tell me she had watched part of the gay block party on TV news. She said, "I thought I might see the two of you there. It looked like they were having a lot of fun." And when my grandmother comes home for holidays we all get together over at my aunt's house, rather than me trying to keep everybody happy by running back and forth between my family and Carole.

For Gary, too, the fact that his parents accept Tod almost as a son represents an important source of strength in their relationship.

My parents include Tod in 99 percent of everything they do that involves me. They like him a lot. Dad is retired and loves to be handy, so he lets Tod tell him what needs to be done around here. He comes in with his own key to putter around during the week when we're not home, or they work together when my folks come for Sunday dinner. Mother and I generally wind up in the kitchen, fixing dinner and talking.

Recently we all went out for dinner with some of my parents' friends, and afterward everyone came back here for coffee. Tod and I referred to ourselves as "we," as we always do, and no one seemed at all uncomfortable.

Both our sets of parents are happily married, and in that sense they serve as role models for us. We hope that eventually Tod's parents will be able to accept us. A large extended family gives you a sense of your roots. Not many gay couples get that kind of stability because they tend to write off their parents as a lost cause instead of trying to work on the communication problems between them.

Tod dreads the crisis that will come when he finally has to tell his folks that he does not plan to come back home after law school, that his future lies with Gary. He has asked himself many times about the consequences of that decision.

Once you say you're gay you can't take it back. If I were to alter my relationship with my parents by letting them know the whole truth, and then if I were to lose Gary for some reason, what would I have left? Nothing. I want the whole pie, my folks and him, too. If they reject him, and in doing so reject me as well, it will mean that for him I've given up everyone else in the world I care about. That's a terrible responsibility to ask anyone to assume.

Tim had the same fears when he first became involved with George. In that case it was not only a question of George's losing parents but of losing his children as well.

If George had been refused visiting rights because of living with me I would have felt that as a heavy responsibility. It's important to me that he have a good relationship with both his kids and his parents; if he should have to give all of them up for me it would be a potential source of resentment that could backfire on us at any time.

Fortunately for everyone, George's parents understood the importance of putting the children's needs first. When his marriage broke up they encouraged their daughter-in-law to visit the two men as a way of assuring herself that visitation with their father and his lover would not harm George's five- and seven-year-old sons. Tim told us how things worked out.

When Eleanor came to meet me we took her out for dinner because we thought it would be easier on her than coming here to the apartment. I tried to be really supportive; I talked about my interest in the kids and showed her that I want to be sensitive to their needs. Later, when we offered to show her the apartment, she liked it a lot. George told her about our lifestyle—that it's normal—no parties every night, no orgies. She decided it would be OK for the kids to visit.

In the meantime, George had talked to his parents on the phone. He asked them if they had some questions about homosexuality, or our relationship in particular, and they were sort of intrigued, so they sent us plane tickets to come and visit them in the Midwest. We decided to take the kids along and Eleanor agreed.

George continued the story.

The kids liked Tim, and showed it. If I held one, the other wanted to be held by him. They were friendlier and more talkative with him than with me, even. Both of my parents seemed relaxed, and they liked Tim's willingness to take over with the kids when the rest of us were busy talking. We really had a good time.

The right of gay parents to visit and in many cases to raise their own children in a homosexual environment has been increasingly affirmed by court decisions over the past several years. Testimony from respected authorities bears out the wisdom of this trend. In 1973, for example, a gay college professor who did not want to lose contact with his three children sought help from Dr. Benjamin Spock, Dr. Judd Marmor, and Dr. Wardell Pomeroy, among others. Dr. Spock responded as follows:

Questions about parental visitation rights and child custody should not be decided, I believe, on the basis of a parent's sexual orientation. They should be decided on such bases as the parent's devotion to his child, his sensibleness in managing the child, evidence of his child's love of him, his general ethical standards.

Every individual's sexual identity has some combination of heterosexual and homosexual trends. Whether he ends up predominantly heterosexual, as a majority do, or predominantly homosexual has nothing to do with his morality.

I know of no evidence that homosexual parents are more apt to raise homosexual children. Most homosexuals are the children of conventionally heterosexual parents.*

Dr. Judd Marmor, later president of the American Psychiatric Association, had this to say:

I know of no evidence that predominantly heterosexual parents are more loving, supportive or stable in their parental roles than homosexual men and women.

The problem is not with the relationship between predominantly homosexual parents and their children, but with a society which has misunderstood and denied human sexuality and most particularly that of persons whose orientation differs from the majority's.

It is true that there is a problem of possible ridicule of children by their peers as a consequence of the public recognition of the homosexual orientation of the parent. A similar problem, however, is faced by any minority group member's child if the family resides among a largely non-minority group. Difference is not easily accepted in our culture, but it is a fact of life. Just as intelligent Black or Jewish parents can help their children to cope with bigotry, so can homosexual parents.†

Dr. Wardell Pomeroy, coauthor of the 1948 and 1953 Kinsey reports, added the following:

To deprive children of seeing their divorced parents . . . is to do them far more harm than any protection they might [thereby] be afforded.

There is no evidence to my knowledge that children of such

* From National Gay Task Force's Gay Parents Support Packet.
† Ibid.

homosexual parents are themselves more likely to become homosexual. Very often, the parent who has the children tries to prohibit the other parent from seeing them, not because of their homosexuality but because they are vindictive and are using the homosexual issue as an excuse for punishing their spouse.*

Lesbian mothers and gay fathers all over the country are fighting to keep their children, and some of them are winning. Generally speaking, state laws do not read in a discriminatory fashion, so that changes of precedent depend on sympathetic, enlightened judges and liberal-minded social service workers. In Portland, Maine, for example, a superior court justice ruled in favor of a thirty-five-year-old mother, stating that her home life "appears to adequately meet the social, psychological, physical and moral needs" of her two children, aged ten and seven. In Morristown, New Jersey, a domestic relations court judge awarded visitation rights to a lesbian mother on the grounds that the rights of homosexual parents are "the same as those of heterosexual parents." And in 1973 an Oregon court of appeals allowed a gay father to retain custody of his two sons, "finding that the boys' welfare was not being adversely affected by living with him."

Many child custody cases are arranged between divorcing parents out of court, of course. Jack Latham has kept his two children off and on since the boy was just a baby and the girl about four. Writing in *Gay Sunshine,*† Latham described some of the joys and restrictions that fatherhood can bring to a gay man. He also commented on the issue of custody:

The sharing Roberta and I do in the care of our children is our arrangement alone. No one has "custody" and everyone has rights. I am incredibly lucky in that, of course. I trust that I will never have to face the issue of whether I am a competent parent on any legal level, though I have to face it daily in every room in the house; each room is a courtroom where my ability

* Ibid.
† *Gay Sunshine,* Spring 1975.

is scrutinized by little people whose opinions are all-important.

But I also know that I have little hope if legal issues are ever raised. I have gone over and over Kenneth Pitchford's lines about his son, that our society will "take him away from my double contamination / as a mothering father whose sickness must surely have poisoned the child by now / ... the afflicted child showing all the damnation-confirming traits by being / imaginative, curious, lively, lovely."

Charlie and Terry, who live with Charlie's two young children in southern California, were asked about the circumstances that led to this arrangement. Charlie said that he had not seen the children since they were babies, but that his wife had recently had marital problems of her own. "She has two more children and felt that the kids would be better off with me, that I could give them a more supportive home life."

Asked whether they hope the children will turn out to be gay, these men gave the same answer that we consistently hear from gay parents. Terry said:

We're trying to rear our children without prejudice of any sort, to any subculture. On a sexual level, whatever they choose to do is fine with us; if they became bisexual, we'd give them the best advice we can. If they become gay or heterosexual, we'll do the same. The important thing to us is that our generation grew up with a lot of hangups, a lot of guilt feelings. Our goal is to try to raise our children so that they will be without hangups. Without guilt. Without problems.

Charlie added, "We personally feel that having children in the home gives a kind of stabilizing effect to our relationship. It gives us something besides a social life outside the home; we consider it to be a real plus for us."

Speaking of a gay parents group they formed when they first got the children, Charlie remarked:

One thing we discovered was that our concerns were those of every other parent. Things like, "I don't like to eat that," "I don't want to go to bed," "I'm sick and I can't go to school," love and affection—you know, it's exactly the same thing as if we were a male and female couple. There are no differences. The mechanics of raising children—whether you take a permissive line or an authoritarian line—is certainly a personal choice. The children are going to react as you react to them. We've been very clear to them about our relationship and the fact that they are as responsible to Terry as they are to me, and as a result they see us both as parent figures. As I said before, the problems we have are no different, the joys we have are no different.

At a meeting of Columbia, Maryland's, Coalition of Gay Sisters where lesbian motherhood was to be the subject of a forum discussion, the chairwoman explained that even though not all of the group were presently living with children, lesbians want to know what to expect if they should ever become involved with a mother. Interestingly enough, any problems directly connected with gay sexuality and the children's response to it were generally discounted. Sometimes, in fact, a need to "tell the children" never arises: "they just seem to know what's going on." As with Charlie and Terry, whom we mentioned earlier, there is little concern over the children's sexual orientation, and most mothers try not to teach sex roles. Boys and girls learn that every kind of skill is appropriate to either sex, that kids can do whatever males or females are supposed to do; "plumbing, cooking, painting, sewing—you learn to do whatever needs to be done."

Several women were quick to point out that there can be advantages, to counterbalance disadvantages, in having two mothers. Female lovers usually take a real interest in the kids. As one woman remarked, "There are things that a father would miss that the second mother picks up every time." Furthermore, there is less ego pressure on the "second mother," so that often she can be more objective about the children. One woman in this position related that she had had occasion to call a school principal about some trouble or other. At first he had been suspicious and wanted to know who she was, and she made the relationship clear. Now he contacts her when possible in preference to the natural mother, who explained, "She's going to act like a person, and I'm going to act like a mother."

Of course, just as when a stepfather or any other non-parent enters the home, certain difficulties are likely to arise. One woman, who characterized herself as a "non-motherly type," expressed real resentment of a teenaged son's interference in her relationship with his mother. She was able to reach some accommodation with the boy by helping him with school projects and taking him fishing, but in the end she had to admit failure. The relationship did not last because the boy won. Her way of putting it was fervently echoed by other members of the group: "You cannot take the mother from the children. There is no way!" Moreover, there was general agreement that in the end this was only right. The kids must be the top priority. Another woman related that she had given up one lover who was also a mother because the demands of the other's two children were interfering with her commitment to her own three. She couldn't give adequate attention to five at once, and the "stepfamily" had to go.

None of the women present was afraid of losing her children, though that subject was raised more than once. As someone said, "Sometimes the fathers want the kids for spite, but if they had them, what would they do with them?" One mother who had recently been through a separation related that her husband had considered stealing his son; his lawyer dissuaded him. Another pointed out that her children had actually gained a father when she was divorced. He had paid very little attention to them when he was living at home, but now that he saw them infrequently he had learned to value their company. In this, as in other aspects of divorce and "remarriage" to a gay lover, we got the impression that lesbian motherhood poses as many issues as motherhood does for a nongay parent trying to raise children in the absence of the natural father. Any adult coming into an already established home has to work out ways of comfortably relating to the mother and each of her children.

Gay men and women who never had children of their own often express an interest in adopting or in serving as foster parents for someone else's rejected offspring. Probably more men than women have had an opportunity to do this, because most homeless young people who have a known history of homosexual behavior are males. For example, a boy who has made a career of hustling is often assumed to be gay, and if there is a question of foster placement, sometimes a sympathetic caseworker will arrange to have a gay man give him a home.

Joseph B., a New Englander who formerly served as headmaster of a private school in the Virgin Islands, has had four foster sons over the years. Keith, who has been with him off and on for five years, is the only one of them who does not consider himself gay. At thirteen the boy was a runaway who had been supporting himself on hustling and bad checks when Joe befriended him in a bus station, giving the boy a home and supervising his education. Keith attended Joe's school in the Virgin Islands and now is a university student. Joe has been approved by the state of Massachusetts as his guardian and foster father, prior to formal adoption.

More and more gay singles and stable couples are considering adoption, particularly in progressive communities. We know two San Francisco men who have adopted a Chilean boy, and many others who are making inquiries about the necessary legal procedures. Enlightened, compassionate social workers will often go out on a limb to help a hard-to-place child find a good home, sometimes by closing their eyes to the fact that the prospective parent is gay, so that some homosexuals have been able to become parents even when official policies would not have permitted it.

Of course, a good number of gay people are married and raising their own children. Some of them are victims of the delusion that marriage can "cure" homosexual tendencies; the greatest number seem to be men who wish to preserve the security and social acceptance that go with a wife and family. Their homosexual needs are met by a series of extramarital affairs, but there is always a price to pay. The married gays we have interviewed are all more or less uncomfortable with their situation. Some feel terribly guilty about betraying their wives. Others are resigned to a superficial marriage and a loveless sex life, because the family-oriented gay man generally finds it difficult to develop meaningful relationships with his lovers. He cannot afford to let his emotions become too deeply involved, and he cannot risk being seen in the company of men who are known to be gay. He may cruise a park or he might frequent a porn movie house that caters to closeted men. Every now and then some error or miscalculation may cause him to be found out, sometimes with tragic results.

In the fall of 1977 there was a fire at the Washington, D.C., Cinema Follies during the 5:30 showing of a gay men's sex film. The fire exits were locked, and nine men died. Some carried no ID because of fear of exposure, but several married men, including a Protestant minister and a Capitol Hill aide, were identified among the victims. In other cases, prominent married men have been mugged and killed in lonely cruising areas, or picked up in raids followed by newspaper coverage and public scandal.

Almost invariably these men turn out to have been true "closet cases," unsuspected by families, colleagues, or friends. The tawdriness of their sex lives is dictated by a desperate need for secrecy. But in many other cases the wives of gay men know, or at least suspect, that their husbands need sexual gratification and emotional relationships with other males.

Frequently such a couple has entered into marriage with

the husband determined to put his homosexual interests behind him and the wife in total ignorance of his attraction to men. As the marriage matures, however, such men often find that they are unwilling, or unable, to forgo male love. Their wives either close their eyes to signs of a furtively conducted private life or, if the relationship is a good one in other ways, they learn to live with the situation. We know one older couple who have sustained an emotionally and financially supportive relationship by having the husband's lover make his home with them. Mrs. X. prefers having a husband who sleeps with his friend in another room to having no husband at all. Both men enjoy her company and she enjoys theirs.

We are also friendly with attorneys Mary and Brice M., both in their late fifties. They have been married for over twenty years, though Brice has always been strictly gay. The daughter of a South Carolina judge, Mary was once married to a straight man and has grandchildren. As she grew older she found that gay men took her more seriously as a person and a professional than did the heterosexual southerners she knew, with their ideals of helpless womanhood. Brice was a friend; he needed a wife for career reasons, and so they undertook a marriage of convenience that neither has regretted. Sexual loyalty is simply irrelevant to the relationship.

A different kind of situation: Laura and Bob are a younger couple with three children. She holds an excellent management position with a major company. Her job requires extensive travel, and he plays the major parent role. For them an open marriage has proved to be the answer; both have lovers outside the home. In still other cases, a wife simply accepts the fact that her husband is bisexually oriented and needs to spend time regularly with men.

The decision to preserve such a marriage is never easy; many wives never get over the bitterness and resentment of not being able to meet their husbands' sexual needs. Where there are children, however, or a social position to maintain, arrangements like these are not at all uncommon.

Relatively few women choose to remain married after discovering that they are happier with a female lover. "Women want a nest," as one of our lesbian friends told us. "In most cases they are not willing to make a charade of marriage." We do know two women who live double lives with husband and lover. Elena, for example, lives in a tightly knit upper-middle-class Italian community and has a partially disabled child. She cannot consider sacrificing him for her own happiness. Elizabeth, on the other hand, has no such excuse. Her children are nearly grown, her husband is a wealthy and prominent professional man, and she herself has a graduate degree. But the thought of losing her considerable social status and exposing her family to scandal outweighs any thoughts of freedom.

Elizabeth agreed to record her story on tape for one of our interviewers.

I think my sexual feelings for men are average. My husband and I make love regularly and though I don't find it thrilling, who does after all these years? I enjoy it as much as most women do, I think. I didn't have much sexual experience before we were married, so I don't have any other men to compare him to. I've never wanted to have an affair with a man. When I've wanted sex outside our marriage it's been with women.

I met S. at a bar in C. many years ago and we've had a relationship ever since. I make excuses for where I'm going; I lie all the time. Actually my husband has a life of his own, too; for all I know he's got a lover. Sometimes I think he assumes I have a man in C. and just lets it go. We just don't discuss it.

I hate my feelings for S. sometimes, for being bisexual. If I could stop it, I would. I think of it as an addiction; some women take pills, some drink, some have affairs with men they care nothing for, and I like women. When I'm with S.'s friends I don't feel as bad. They seem to feel it's the most natural thing in the world, it's a whole different generation. I just can't think that way. I was brought up to view lesbians as filthy, perverted, and I've never really gotten over that. Sometimes on my way home from C. I think I ought to drive off the road, just kill myself, so I won't be so divided up, and so no one will have to suffer anymore because of me.

Even though I don't know you very well, I wanted to tell you my story because I want the world to know what's going on. Maybe someone reading this book will feel better knowing she's not alone, that other people share her affliction.

My advice to a young person who's bisexual? Well, I'd tell them to make up their minds, do one or the other, but don't try to do both. If they've got the nerve and the kind of personality that can cope with it, they could decide to be gay. Or if they're more old-fashioned, they could find a person of the opposite sex whom they love and give that a try. Given my background, I think I've done the best I could. I'd do it again. But young people these days have a better chance, they don't have all the hangups, so I think it would be easier for them.

Ideally, the younger generation, for whom sexuality is an area of greater freedom, will be better able to organize their lives in the direction of self-realization and joy. As parents, we hope so. Our gay children and friends are some of the most joyful people we know.

Gays and Religion

We are people of God and whoever we may be
We have freedom from the bondage of guilt.
We are warmed in the sunshine of saintly company,
We are members of the Church Christ has built.

*Fellowship Hymn of the Metropolitan Community
Church by the Reverend Michael England
(Traditional Irish Melody)*

One of the most difficult problems confronting some parents in accepting our children's homosexuality stems from our religious beliefs. Our churches have consistently taught us that homosexuality is a sin. How are we to deal with this when we find that our daughter or son is gay? Some parents have qualms about their children's indulgence in evil or sinful practices. Others simply use church doctrine as an excuse for not dealing with their own feelings about having reared a homosexual child; they continue to harass the child on "religious" grounds rather than seeking constructive ways of handling the problem.

For parents who want to learn why homosexuality is anathema to traditionally informed Christians and Jews, as well as about liberalizing trends in contemporary religious thought, there are some good and valid answers. In this chapter we address the issues primarily from the viewpoint and experience of gay women and men; our children have been subject to the same teachings and attitudes as we, and many of them have been as deeply troubled as we are. So the answers are the same for all of us. We believe that this chapter provides at least some of those answers, drawn largely from the opinions of informed clergy seeking to help lay women and men retain their faith in religious institutions and in the love of God.

Many gay people feel that they need the support of an organized religious community, whether or not they choose to identify themselves openly as homophiles. Having grown up believing that God accepts you when no one else will, a high proportion of gays are interested in maintaining religious ties. This is evidenced, for example, in the columns on religion that appear frequently in the gay press from coast to coast. Here are excerpts from the first in a series of articles entitled "Why Religion . . . Why Not?" by Brian McNaught.*

Why religion?
Why should a man who was fired by a Catholic paper, refused entrance into the Jesuits, declared a heretic by one theologian and condemned to hell by another all because he is gay, write about religion to other gay men and women who have been mercilessly persecuted and ostracized by organized religious bodies? Why should a gay publication print such a column?
Not to do so would be pure idiocy.
Despite the fact that most gay women and men I have talked with have left the institutional Church, they all continue to remain in its tight grasp. Even if they have discarded the concept of God, there is an inner turmoil which cries for peace.
The Jews and Saint Paul thought that all persons were born heterosexual . . . that persons engaging in homosexual acts were heterosexuals who were deviating from the norm. They saw it

* *Blade*, July 1976, p. 7.

as a matter of choice. Constitutional homosexuals have made no choice. How can there be sin?

Knowing that every time they engage in sexual activity they break a commandment traditional to every Judeo-Christian doctrine, many gay people try to continue a relationship with the congregation of their choice at the price of being cut off from every deep human involvement. Father John J. McNeill, a Jesuit priest who psychologically identifies with homosexuals even though he himself maintains vows of celibacy, describes the dilemma of the religiously committed homosexual this way:

[Such men and women are] deprived of their potentialities for growth and development in their personal self-identity ... not to mention their agonies of guilt, remorse, self-hatred, and potential emotional breakdown when they fail to achieve the accepted goal.

Total and unending sexual abstinence attained without severe emotional disorders, and even mental breakdowns, is a practical and successful goal of counselling only in a minority of cases.

A majority of counsellors and confessors find that the traditional guidelines [advising celibacy] are no longer adequate but, on the contrary, frequently lead to serious harm and destruction for their penitents or patients.*

As parents we seek to promote the integration of gay men and women into all social institutions. And membership in a religious community is one of the most important facets of this integration.

The homosexual suffers great mental anguish and a profound sense of alienation, often believing himself to be an outcast not only from human society but from divine love as well. The person with a homosexual orientation tends to accept his homosexuality as his deepest self-identity image, the most important single fact about himself, because he tends to accept his image from the attitudes of the people about him.

* McNeill, *The Church and the Homosexual*, p. 154.

Homosexuals will never master their sexual drive in a positive way and integrate it successfully into their whole personality development until they become aware of themselves as persons of infinite dignity and worth, worthy of their fellow humans' respect and consideration.*

Father McNeill believes that gay people have a unique gift of spirituality that permits them to contribute something special to the spiritual development of all human beings. To support his thesis he quotes the famous psychoanalyst Karl Jung: "He [the homosexual] is endowed with a wealth of religious feelings which help him to bring the *ecclesia spiritualis* into reality, and a spiritual receptivity which makes him responsive to revelation."†

McNeill observes that "in those cultures where the 'machismo' image reigns, religious prayer and worship are considered activities fit only for women. The homosexual [on the other hand] can be free from a need for violence and dedicated to the quest of peace. . . . Each of the special qualities Jung attributes to the homosexual community is usually considered as a striking characteristic of Christ—the qualities which distinguished him from the ordinary man."‡

Of course it is not only within Christian denominations that gay people are having difficulty finding acceptance today; Jewish gays may have particular difficulty achieving self-acceptance and recognition within their spiritual community, for it was in the writings of the ancient Hebraic fathers that the taboo against homosexual love was first explicitly codified. Old Testament laws are frequently invoked to condemn the "abomination" of sodomy.

In preparing this chapter, we began with the understanding that we are not theologians. We have drawn heavily on published sources and have relied on interviews with

* Ibid.
† Ibid., p. 144.
‡ Ibid., p. 145.

priests, rabbis, and Protestant ministers to find out how clergy and their congregations view the homosexual experience in our time. We have also talked with many, many gay men and women whose deeply felt desire to retain meaningful religious values has driven them to seek God in spite of having frequently encountered rejection in the churches and synagogues they attended as children.

We regret that so many of the heartfelt confessions of faith we have received from friends cannot be included in this book. Space permits us to include only a tiny fraction of this rich material. For ourselves, having the opportunity to talk with so many devout gay men and women and to witness the joy they feel at being close to God has been a moving and rewarding experience. It has also been an unhappy one at times; we have felt deep compassion for the many whose rejection by trusted religious leaders and church officials has left them in despair, sometimes bordering on the suicidal.

Over the past several years a growing number of clergymen of all denominations have been struggling with the "problem" of homosexuality and concluding that the problem has been generated by their own ignorance and bias. They have looked into the Bible and into their own hearts and found that God has no trouble loving gays. They acknowledge that now it is up to them, as messengers of God's word, to go and do likewise. Though churches have failed in the past to understand and communicate God's love to these children, they must no longer do so. Increasing numbers of concerned priests, ministers, and rabbis are taking up that cause.

Here are some of the discoveries that particularly excited us in our study of Judeo-Christian religious teachings and what we understand them to mean to Jewish and Christian believers today. We begin with the Book of Genesis.

When Lot left the home of his uncle Abraham, he settled

in Sodom, where God had resolved to send two angels to evaluate the extent of wickedness and sinfulness. Guided by Abraham, they were met at the gates by Lot, who saw that they had no shelter for the night and who urged them to accept his hospitality. Before they retired, the house was beset by local residents demanding that the strangers be brought out to them so that they might "know" them. Lot refused to allow this, even offering to produce his daughters as proof that he intended to stand firm. The crowd was thwarted in the end by the angels themselves, who smote the people with blindness. The next morning, Lot and his family left the city with the angels, and God overthrew it with fire and brimstone from heaven.

The traditional conception of the sin of Sodom arises from the fact that the word here translated as *know* (*yādha'*) is used by itself in ten places in the Old Testament to denote heterosexual coition. In five additional texts it is used in conjunction with *mishkābh* (in this context, "to lie") to mean the same thing. But *yādha'* appears by itself no less than 943 times in a nonsexual connotation, according to F. Brown, et al., in *A Hebrew and English Lexicon of the Old Testament* (Oxford, 1952).

There is no Old Testament text in which *yādha'* refers to homosexual coitus, with the single exception of this disputed Sodom and Gomorrah story in Genesis. The less ambiguous word *shākhabh*, however, is used for both homosexual and bestial intercourse, in addition to coition between man and woman. *Shākhabh* appears fifty times in the Old Testament; if it had been used instead of *yādha'* in the Sodom story, the meaning of the text would have been unmistakable. As it is, we have no grounds to assume that the wrath of the Almighty was turned against these cities because homosexual practices occurred there.

An alternate theory has been developed by biblical scholars. Since *yādha'* commonly means "to get acquainted with," the demand to "know" the visitors may well have implied some serious breach of the rules of hospitality. Several considerations provide support for this view.

In the first place, Lot was not a native of Sodom, but had the status of a resident alien, or *gēr*. As such, he may not have had the right to admit unidentified foreigners to the city. City gates were closed at night expressly to prevent lawless or subversive aliens from entering on unknown errands, and travelers carried credentials because they might at any time be asked to prove that they were abroad on legitimate business. Thus we might translate "Bring them out to us, that we may know them" as "We wish to know whom you are bringing as guests into our city." Lot's refusal to turn his visitors over to this horde of vigilantes is totally in keeping with the contemporary laws of etiquette, because in those days no civic police force protected strangers in a city. Any kind of robbery or physical abuse could have been meted out to the two angels if he had agreed to surrender them, but in his home they were safe. He was obliged to protect them as honored guests. It is certain that the Sodomites were demanding he violate the code of hospitality, but not at all clear from the text that they were inclined to indulge in homosexual acts.*

The folklore of various other peoples includes many variations on the biblical story of the destruction of Sodom. Several of these have been noted by scholars. Their common elements include a wicked community which is visited by strangers who are generally divine beings. They are given shelter by humble citizens after having been denied hospitality elsewhere; the city is then destroyed and only the kind hosts are saved. None of these legends indicate that sexual

---

* In any case, Sodom and Gomorrah did not survive long. Geologists tell us that the Five Cities of the Plain were situated on an active fault, where rocks are under tension from being pulled apart by convective forces beneath the surface. A massive earthquake destroyed the Five Cities during biblical times, and unchecked fires accompanied them. The Dead Sea now covers the ruined Bedouin settlements that were once Sodom and Gomorrah.

sins were common in the offending community; general
wickedness and refusal of hospitality form the central
theme of each legend. It would appear that the association
of homosexual practice with the sins of Sodom was a late
addition to biblical lore, which has persisted because we
now define sodomy as a male, principally homosexual act.

Nowhere in all biblical references to Sodom, in fact, is
there any implication that homosexuality was practiced
there. On the contrary, in Ezekiel 16:49–50 we read:
"Behold, this was the iniquity of thy sister Sodom; pride,
fulness of bread, and prosperous ease . . . ; And they were
haughty, and committed abomination [*tō'ēbhāh,* usually
signifying idolatry] before me: therefore I took them away
as I saw good."

It is also significant that none of the biblical condemna-
tions of homosexual behavior (Lev. 18:22, 20:13; Rom.
1:26–27; 1 Cor. 6:9–10; 1 Tim. 1:10) make reference to
Sodom. Of course the Hebraic fathers, and later Saint Paul,
taught that homosexual love was a sin, as was any kind of
sexual intercourse outside marriage and not directed primarily toward the birth of legitimate children. These policies were adopted in about the eighth century B.C., during
the period of Babylonian exile, when maintenance of strong
families was vitally important to the survival of the Jewish
nation. Licentious fornication, including that between males
or females, was associated with idolatrous cults and could
have no place in Judaic, or later in Christian, observance.
For example, in Leviticus 23:22: "Thou shalt not lie with
mankind, as with womankind: it is abomination" (*tō'ēbhāh,*
signifying idolatry). But the threat of wholesale destruction,
as of Sodom, in retribution for homosexual behavior is
found nowhere in the Old or New Testament.

It is because we now have the English word *sodomy,*
which we commonly define as a homosexual act, that so
many biblical passages appear to condemn it. In Kings 13:7
and four other passages we find the English translation of

gedhēshīm (temple servants, some of whom practiced sexual acts in pagan fertility ceremonies) as *sodomites:* "In his efforts to stamp out idolatry, Josiah . . . brake down the houses of the sodomites [*gedhēshīm*] that were in the house of the Lord." In Deuteronomy 23:17–18: "There shall be no harlot of the daughters of Israel, neither shall there be a sodomite [*gādēsh*] of the sons of Israel." The implication is one of forbidden sexual practice, but not specifically between women or between men.

Our Catholic and Protestant sources agree that "homosexual activity between men is proscribed in Leviticus for the same reason that it is in Deuteronomy and Kings I; it is an 'abomination' because of its connection with the fertility rites of the Canaanites. The condemnation of homosexual activity in Leviticus is not an ethical judgment. Homosexuality here is condemned on account of its association with idolatry."*

Christ Himself never mentioned homosexuality. As for the sin of Sodom, Luke 10:10–13 tells of Jesus' warning that destruction would fall upon communities where His messengers were not well received. "But whenever you come to a town and they do not welcome you, go out into the open streets and say, 'The very dust of your town that sticks to our feet we wipe off in protest. But understand this: The Kingdom of God is at hand.' I tell you, on that day Sodom will fare better than that town!" Here again, the message is of ungodliness associated with inhospitality to strangers.

The Apostle Paul preached and wrote during the period of Nero and Caligula, when an appalling degree of licentiousness characterized Roman society. Male and female prostitution, sexual abuse of slaves, child molestation, and diversionary homosexual liaisons on the part of hetero-

---

* Kosnik, Anthony, et al., *Human Sexuality: New Directions in American Catholic Thought.* A study commissioned by The Catholic Theological Society of America (New York: Paulist Press, 1977), p. 190.

sexuals were common. Violence and dehumanization accompanied the exercise of every imaginable type of sexual caper.

Paul condemned all aspects of sexual license, assuming as he did that the possibility of choice was present for everyone. He knew nothing of sexual orientation as a basic trait of the adult personality and saw no way to control sexual abuses but by rooting sexual expression firmly within the context of formal Christian marriage. To quote again from the Catholic Theological Society of America's committee report on human sexuality: "St. Paul is not speaking here at all of the true homosexual for whom the 'natural' use of sex creates not only an aversion but even, in some cases, an impossibility. [He] has been interpreted as speaking here only of those who *deliberately* [sic] choose homosexual over heterosexual relations."*

By the time of Paul's conversion the sin of Sodom had become widely identified among Jews with homosexual behavior. Philo of Alexandria (c. 13 B.C.–c. A.D. 50) was evidently the first author to connect the destruction of that city with the practice whose name it now bears, although some late second or early first century B.C. apocryphal documents had strongly suggested it. Paul's New Testament teachings, as well as Christian tradition and legislation thereafter, were strongly influenced by that later interpretation.

The moral writing of nearly all the fathers of the Church in the first two centuries after Christ was dominated by the Stoic philosophical doctrines which were popular at that time. The concept of "natural law" was central to these doctrines; Stoic philosophers taught that any sexual act unrelated to procreation is an offense against nature and reason. This view was later incorporated by Saint Thomas Aquinas into his version of natural law. He regarded

* Ibid., p. 195.

masturbation, sodomy, and bestiality (in that order of gravity) as sins *contra natura*, therefore more seriously unchaste than adultery, incest, or fornication.

All these prohibitions were directed principally against "unnatural" acts committed by males.

An anomaly within the Christian tradition ... is the double standard that prevailed with regard to homosexual acts performed by women. Although ... St. Thomas treats them as equally serious, the medieval penitentials, Church legislation, and Christian tradition in general penalize homosexual acts by men with uncommon severity, while virtually disregarding those by women. An explanation for the inequity ... seems to lie ... in the sexist androcentrism [central importance of the male] of the West and reverence for semen that borders on superstition. Ignorant of human physiology and dependent on medical philosophers of antiquity, the Fathers of the Church and medievals after them looked upon the male sperm as something "almost human."*

We have referred several times to the work of Father Anthony Kosnik and his committee. Their study, *Human Sexuality: New Directions in American Catholic Thought,* grew out of the liberal thought that was encouraged among theologians during the papacy of John XXIII, the era of Vatican II.

Pope John had established a Papal Commission for the Study of Population, the Family and Birth in 1964. In its majority report the commission rejected the traditional view that sexuality must be directed solely toward the production of children and emphasized instead the human person as the integrating center of moral values. Moreover, the commission explicitly recognized that personal and interpersonal values lie at the core of human sexuality; to be valid, these must contribute to the growth and development of the person.

Paul VI became Pope not long after the Vatican II

* Ibid., p. 198.

document was published. He repudiated the commission's recommendations, indicating that sex must first and foremost serve the procreative function. But the doors opened during Vatican II were not to be so easily shut again.

The diversity of responses received from various Episcopal Conferences, the theological ferment which followed upon the encyclical and a host of recent surveys of clergy and faithful indicate that there remains a wide divergence between official Church teaching and the actual practice of the faithful. . . . Among the factors that helped influence this profound change in attitudes and practice [is] an increased sense of personal freedom and responsibility for the determination of one's own life that has made the uncritical conformity to authoritative pronouncements an unacceptable response.*

In 1972 the board of directors of the Catholic Theological Society of America commissioned the comprehensive study of human sexuality from which we have been quoting. This was prepared by three priests; a sister who specializes in patristics—the study of the Church fathers—as well as in spirituality and women in the Church; a married layman who is a psychologist, a theologian, and a trial lawyer. One of the priests completed his doctoral studies with a thesis on child-free marriage. The chairman, Anthony Kosnik, is professor of moral theology and dean at Saints Cyril and Methodius Seminary; his doctorate was in sacred theology.

An extensive treatment of homosexuality was included in their study, and thus we continue to quote directly from that work to explain contemporary liberalizing trends in American Catholic thought. The Kosnik report, however, has not been accepted as official Church doctrine.

The committee began by noting that

for too long homosexuals have been the victims not only of misunderstanding but also of silence and neglect on the part of theologians and those charged with pastoral care within the

* Ibid., pp. 48–49.

Church. . . . Particularly for people not altogether secure in their own sexual identity, homosexuality is a highly emotional subject, not easily permitting of concrete objective discussion. Even among those self-assured, outright ignorance often gives rise to irrational fears of homosexual persons. What gross unfairness can be committed, for example, by those who see all homosexuals as child molesters or constituents of some subversive underground.*

Having explored the historical and theological rationale for a traditionally based condemnation of homosexual behavior, as reported in a previous section, the Committee on the Study of Human Sexuality went on to develop a series of pastoral reflections intended to serve as guidelines for modern ministry to homosexuals. A pertinent selection:

An experienced pastor or spiritual director knows that absolute continence is ultimately a grace of God, not given to all. Where it apparently has not been given, no alternative remains for the pastoral minister but to accept the homosexual condition as a given and to assist the homosexual to live a life in accord with the same moral standards as heterosexuals, striving for the same goals of creativity and integration.†

The committee explains that morally valid sexual expression can exist between a devoted monogamous couple of any gender. Where two people try to love each other selflessly, with mutual caring, the resultant atmosphere of sharing and trust promotes personal growth and development. Promiscuous, exploitative sexual encounters they judge to be mutually destructive and hence immoral. Thus a monogamous couple who share a mutually rewarding sex life may receive absolution and the sacrament of the Eucharist in good conscience. On the other hand, the gay woman or man who enters sexual relationships casually, never developing a true concern for the well-being of the other, is in a state

* Ibid., p. 187.
† Ibid., pp. 216–17.

of sin. No amount of confession can produce a state of grace for the gay Catholic who habitually changes sexual partners for mere physical gratification.

A substantial number of individual priests and Church officials now adhere to this point of view. For example, while preparing material for this chapter we talked with a Jesuit priest who teaches and conducts student counseling at a Catholic college in Maryland. We asked him about his responses to homosexuals whose confessions he hears, and for whom he bears the responsibility of granting absolution. Father W. told us that the role of a pastor is to help the practicing Catholic develop his or her conscience. Persons who are trying to do so to the best of their ability must be treated with compassion and Christian love—the pastor does not help anyone reach God by condemning his or her individual progress toward that goal. The Committee on Human Sexuality agrees.

All else being equal, a homosexual engaging in homosexual acts in good conscience has the same rights of conscience and the same rights to the sacraments as a married couple practicing birth control in good conscience.*

A pastor or counsellor should attempt to help a homosexual make a moral judgment upon his or her relationships and actions in terms of whether or not they are self-liberating, other-enriching, honest, faithful, life-serving, and joyous.†

The Catholic Church has a long, proud tradition of promoting social justice and censuring acts of discrimination. Championing the civil rights of homosexuals is seen to be a morally proper position for the Church in America today.

The traditional Christian attitude toward homosexuality down the centuries makes the Church responsible at least indirectly for much of the prejudice and discrimination that homosexuals

* Ibid., p. 216.
† Ibid., pp. 214–15.

suffer in society today. As representatives of Jesus Christ, Church leaders have a serious responsibility to work toward the elimination of injustices that continue to be perpetrated on homosexuals by society. This includes discriminatory practices in both housing and employment. Particularly in the sphere of legislation and civil rights, Church leadership would do well to follow the lines set down by the Westminster Report commissioned by the former Catholic Archbishop of London, Bernard Cardinal Griffin (1956): "Penal sanctions are not justified for the purpose of attempting to restrain sins against sexual morality committed in private by responsible adults."*

Recognition of a person's civil rights is often the first step toward recognizing his or her right to human dignity and the respect of the community at large. We saw this happen in the case of Jewish and black Americans. And the Church is certainly doing its part in this direction. In the fall of 1976 the following statement was issued by the Catholic bishops of the United States at their semiannual meeting: "Homosexuals, like everyone else, should not suffer from prejudice against their basic human rights. They have a right to respect, friendship and justice. They should have an active role in the Christian community."

And the Washington State Catholic Conference stated its position in March of 1977: "We ... realize that many people have physiological or psychological sexual orientations which are not consonant with the majority and which are beyond their own free choice. We sincerely believe that to discriminate against this group of men and women is not only contrary to sound religious principles but in conflict with protection of basic rights in our American civil life."

We wish we could tell you that every church official and individual clergyman supports this progressive and enlightened attitude toward homosexuals. Such is not yet the case. Change comes slowly to large, long-established institutions, and is often met by resistance and fear. Homosexuality is

* Ibid., pp. 217–18.

seldom discussed from the pulpit, and clergy are often loath to take an unpopular position, even if they have personally achieved an enlightened understanding of a controversial issue. Feeling either unworthy or unwelcome, and frequently both, gays of all religious persuasions often abandon their faith.

Along with the recognition that homosexual persons need and deserve a place in religious communities comes the inevitable question of admitting them to the ministries of various denominations. Homosexual rabbis, priests, and ministers can provide special help to the gay Jew or Christian who seeks to integrate his or her sexuality with faith in God. Heretofore, only closeted gays could hope to follow that vocation. But in the Catholic and Episcopal churches, progress is clearly being made in that direction.

The Committee on Human Sexuality reasoned as follows:

> In the case of a person exclusively or predominately homosexual and contemplating entry into the priesthood or religious life ... candidates should be confident that they can live the ideals and expectations of a celibate life. . . . All the requirements and expectations made of heterosexual priests and religious hold for homosexual inclinations as well. . . . [But] homosexuals should never be encouraged to enter the seminary or the religious novitiate simply as an escape from confronting their sexuality and making it a creative force in their lives.*

As to the practical application of these views, we ourselves do not know of any openly gay persons who have been admitted to the Catholic priesthood or religious life, though we do know of several who were dismissed from seminary in connection with their professed gay identity.

The Episcopal bishop of New York, however, ordained a lesbian priest early in 1977. Participating in the decision to do so were the eight-member Standing Committee of the Diocese of New York, a proposing rector and vestry, the

* Ibid., p. 217.

Ministries Commission, a screening conference of clergy and laity, a seminary faculty, a psychiatrist, and the bishop himself.

The Right Reverend Paul Moore, Jr., who ordained Ellen Marie Barrett, was hotly criticized from many quarters for his action on her behalf. The following excerpts from his statement of rebuttal to that criticism provide a superb summation of our own views about Christ's message to humanity.

On Monday, December 15, 1975, I ordained Ellen Marie Barrett a Deacon, and on Monday, January 10, 1977, I ordained her a Priest. I acted in full knowledge of her professed homosexual orientation, believing (as I still do) that she was fully qualified in every way for holy orders.

Her recommendation from The General Theological Seminary was excellent in terms of character, personality, behavior and academic competence.

The fact that she had publicly admitted her homosexual orientation was not judged by the Bishop or the Standing Committee to be a barrier to ordination. All of us were aware that many homosexual persons have been ordained into the ministry of the Church over the years and have served the Church well. They were, of course, forced to be very secretive about this aspect of their personality. Now it is possible to be more open about one's sexual orientation, and that is a healthy development.

The personal morality, lifestyle and behavior of every ordained must be and is carefully weighed by the Bishop, the Ministries Commission, and the Standing Committee. This applies to persons of all sexual orientations. In the absence of public scandal, however, the personal morality of an ordained becomes . . . a matter between him or her and a confessor, pastor or bishop. Suffice it to say that Ellen Barrett's life and profession had not been an occasion of public scandal.

Her ordination was not a political act and did not seek to make a statement about homosexual activity; it was, like any ordination, the solemn laying on of hands upon a person carefully and prayerfully chosen.

A great many people who opposed this ordination shared

with me some of their theological views; I should respond in kind. . . . I believe that better guidance will be found in the fullness of the Gospel than in the narrowness of isolated verses selected painstakingly from the Epistles or the Old Testament. There is timelessness to the message of God's love that outweighs the datedness of so many Biblical injunctions rooted in ancient societies.

There has . . . been decided movement in the Church away from a tradition which grudgingly accepted sex for procreative ends only toward a more encompassing, psychosomatic view of sexuality as a good and desirable way of expressing a loving relationship between persons.

In shifting away from an exclusively procreative view of sex to one of sex as a human expression of love, we move beyond explicit Biblical guidance. I pray that the Holy Spirit will guide us. The Church has reawakened to the realization that Truth is an open-ended process of progressive revelation, and what we are witnessing in our time with regard to human sexuality is just such a process.

For most people, however, this rethinking of the morality of sexual expression is not yet to be extended to homosexual persons. I believe that their recognition as full members of the Church with the opportunities, rights, and responsibilities of all other members is based ultimately on Jesus' view of human nature as reflected in the Gospel. Again and again, He broke through the prejudices of the day to accept and lift up those rejected and downgraded by others. And just as the reasons for their rejection were often beyond their control, so the homosexual person's condition is generally not a matter of conscious choice.

The forces that shape sexual orientation are still somewhat mysterious, but there is general agreement that our sexuality is forged at an incredibly early age, long before puberty. Thus, a person's sexual preference is not in the category of sin, and the sometimes violent social prejudice against the homosexual condition comes painfully close to the recorded targets of Jesus' preaching.

In recent years an increasing number of Protestant churches have dealt with the issue of homosexuality. During the summer of 1977, Presbyterians, Unitarians, and the United Church of Christ all announced support for the gay cause.

Delegates to the Sixteenth Annual General Assembly of the continental Unitarian Universalists, representing over one thousand member societies, took official action to express solidarity with the gay community in its continuing struggle for dignity and individual civil rights. The delegation overwhelmingly ratified a bylaw amendment enjoining member societies from exercising discrimination based on "affectional or sexual orientation" and adopted a general resolution calling for resistance to the type of tactic used in Dade County, Florida, to repeal a gay rights ordinance in June of 1977. There was virtually no opposition to these measures. A resolution on human rights for gays, proposed by the association's Gay Caucus and adopted during the final session, read in part: "THEREFORE BE IT RESOLVED THAT: The General Assembly of the Unitarian Universalist Association calls on all Unitarian Universalists to use their efforts to stop biased persecution and intolerance of the gay minority."

In July of 1977 the General Synod of the United Church of Christ also passed a resolution deploring "the use of scripture to generate hatred and the violation of civil rights of gay and bisexual persons" in the Dade County referendum campaign. This resolution, which was supported by some 90 percent of the 703 delegates, urged church members to "work for the enactment of civil rights legislation at the federal, state and local levels of government." The United Church of Christ, with 1.8 million members, is considered to be one of the most liberal Protestant denominations.

The United Presbyterian Church, representing 2.6 million members, voted at an annual meeting to retain their task force on the study of homosexuality and possible ordination of gay ministers. The task force had been set up in

1976, and its report to be presented to the assembly in 1978.*
And the General Assembly of the Presbyterian Church in
the United States, also known as the Southern Presbyterian
Church, passed a resolution calling on the church to stand
for equal rights for homosexuals and launched its own two-
year study of homosexuality. The assembly rejected a pro-
posal to brand homosexuality or homosexual practices a sin,
but did say that homosexuality "falls short of God's plan"
for sexual practices.

In general, churches with extensive membership in the
Midwest and South are less tolerant of homosexuality than
their northern or western counterparts. In June of 1976 the
Ohio Conference of the United Church of Christ rejected a
resolution that would have allowed gays to become members of the church and its ministry. As early as 1972, however, the Northern California Conference of that same
church ordained Bill Johnson as the first avowed homosexual minister of an established denomination.

Nonetheless, even among more conservative groups,
change seems to be in the wind. In the fall of 1977, the
General Assembly of the Christian Church (Disciples of
Christ, 1.3 million members) rejected a resolution that
would have condemned homosexuality as an alternate life-
style. The vote was 2,304 to 1,538, after an extensive debate during which a member of the church's voting board
read a moving letter from her homosexual son asking that
his parents neither judge him nor feel guilty about his sexual
preference. A resolution calling for laws to "end the denial
of civil rights and the violation of civil liberties for reasons
of sexual orientation or preference" was passed by the assembly. The resolution further stated that homosexuals are
victims of discrimination and that sodomy laws are unfairly
and unevenly applied against them. The measure admitted
that the church had contributed to the persecution of homo-

---

* It was presented to the assembly in 1978—a report *recommending
ordination*—and was turned down by the majority.

sexuals and should now support legal reform concerning their civil rights.

Methodists have traditionally been among the most conservative of Protestant denominations. The General Conference of the United Methodist Church, meeting in Portland, Oregon, early in 1976, voted overwhelmingly to retain its 1972 Statement of Social Principles rather than substitute a liberalized version that was offered in its place. The Statement of Social Principles reads as follows:

Homosexuals no less than heterosexuals are persons of sacred worth, who need the ministry and guidance of the church in their struggles for human fulfillment, as well as the spiritual and emotional care of a fellowship which enables reconciling relationships with God, with others and with self. Further we insist that all persons are entitled to have their human and civil rights insured, though we do not condone the practice of homosexuality and consider this practice to be incompatible with Christian teaching.

No statement by an official church body represents the views of all members, and the Methodist statement given above provides a case in point. In January of 1977 the Reverend Doctor Edward W. Bauman, pastor of the Foundry United Methodist Church in Washington, D.C., said that the Methodists' official policy declaring homosexuality contrary to Christian principles is a serious mistake and that the church should be a place where gay people are welcome. He told his congregation, in a sermon that was incorporated in a nationally syndicated television series on love and marriage, that extensive readings on the subject of homosexuality and the plight of gay people in America had changed his position "drastically" from one of misunderstanding to a strong feeling of support for change in previous thinking both within and outside of his church. Since the sermon was broadcast on many local TV stations and on the U.S. Armed Forces Network, Dr. Bauman's point of view undoubtedly reached many thousands of Methodists who knew nothing about the official social principles of their church.

Religious denominations that adhere to a literal interpretation of biblical texts still hold firmly to the view that homosexuality is an unacceptable orientation. Delegates to the 1976 Southern Baptist convention also took a strongly negative position; a resolution that was adopted almost unanimously condemned "the practice of homosexuality as sin." It called on the almost thirty-five thousand Baptist churches "not to afford the practice of homosexuality any degree of approval through ordination, employment, or other designations of a normal lifestyle." And in a letter to the *National Enquirer* of April 19, 1977, President L. Duane Brown of the American Council of Christian Churches was quoted as saying, "The history of homosexuals is that they never practice homosexuality alone. They prey on people. That is why we have laws in our communities to protect us from people like them."

Since condemnation of homosexual practice is so clearly called for in the Old Testament, it has been particularly difficult for Jews to accept it as a positive way of loving. But in recent years an increasing awareness that gays form a sizable minority in every part of American society has made Reform Jews uncomfortably aware of the parallels between their own history of persecution and the discrimination routinely practiced against gay people. Jewish liberals and their spiritual leaders have been compelled by their consciences to examine the issue carefully and to question values that are based more on tradition than on rational thought.

An effort to think rationally, keeping in mind the understanding that one's original attitudes were developed from custom and hearsay rather than firsthand knowledge, can sometimes bring about amazing changes. The Reverend Bauman, the Methodist minister from Washington, D.C., had that experience; when we spoke with Rabbi David Goldstein of Baltimore, he told us of an experience similar to the Reverend Bauman's.

The rabbi had realized that homosexuality was becoming such a prominent and controversial issue that he felt obliged to look into it himself, to affirm or reject the views he had been taught during his religious training. The recent summary dismissal of a respected Hebrew teacher who had come out to his superiors also preyed on his mind; he suspected that some injustice had taken place. So Rabbi Goldstein devised a title for a sermon—"Jewish Homosexuals: Outrage or Outcry"—and he announced that it would be delivered in a week's time.

That week he devoted to a crash course in homosexual orientation. The rabbi talked to some Jewish gays. He read Laura Hobson's fictionalized account of her own adjustment to having a gay son. And he studied some recent articles from professional journals, among them one by Dr. Judd Marmor, former president of the American Psychiatric Association and a strong defender of homosexuality as a healthy alternative to the majority preference.

When he wrote his sermon on Friday morning, Rabbi Goldstein began by confessing his presumption in undertaking to address a subject about which he had been completely ignorant. We have selected some passages from that sermon which we feel are especially pertinent:

I was unschooled in this subject, with little or no experience or understanding regarding homosexuality, and no particular insights to bring to bear. I was a product of a society and its Jewish sub-culture, which has systematically abused homosexuals through scorn and ridicule and virtual excommunication.

Why were these days [of writing the sermon] so difficult for me? Because they represented a time of growth, mixed with regret as to my own previous insensitivity. And the two, growth and regret, are painful. I read everything available to me on the subject, although I have only scratched the surface. And, I spoke with several individuals in the Jewish community, who entrusted their confidence in me, and whose anguished expressions helped to further sensitize me to what has been for many of them a nightmare of pain and suffering almost beyond description.

The rabbi said he had discovered that

because we can't or won't deal with them rationally, we badger them into hiding, and even, and perhaps especially, we Jews, because of our ethnic conditioning, tend to relegate Jewish homosexuals to the social and psychological dark alleyway of perverseness and degeneracy.

Many of them, I have found in these turbulent days, are proud, intelligent, often creative and talented people who want desperately to be accepted by the community and make a contribution to it. But they are unable to because in order to do so they must live a lie. They must cloak their homosexuality in secrecy. In many instances, not because they are ashamed of it, but because they are uncertain what effect that knowledge will have upon others.

In Los Angeles there is a Reform synagogue of mostly homosexual members, recently established, and last year taken into the Union of American Hebrew Congregations. [Its name means, in English] "The House of New Life.". . . While I . . . am not at all convinced that there should be separate homosexual congregations, I do understand the forces that brought [this synagogue] into existence in its separateness.

In the words of Rabbi Erwin Herman, who helped to found that synagogue: "The synagogue is that place where [Jewish gays] want to feel the warmth of life, of love, of sharing with their fellow Jews. Yet it is difficult at best to bring their own perceptions of the warmth of life, of love and of sharing into existing synagogues without fear of ridicule and isolation." I believe that our role as Jews in this debate is clear. For our heritage is not limited to . . . the outrage of the Biblical authors of the Book of Leviticus. Out of the long centuries of our wandering and suffering, I believe we should have learned something about the evils some societies have perpetrated in the name of established belief or opinion. We Jews above all, who have suffered so much from the iron men who knew only one truth, who could tolerate only one way of living, their way of living, we of all people, should respond to the cry of the homosexual community; for an end to discrimination and oppression, and for a new perception of their plight.

The first church to be totally organized around the needs of gay people was founded by the Reverend Troy Perry, who had been a Pentecostal minister for four years before he understood that he was homosexual. To be ordained in his church, marriage was a requirement; the Reverend Perry had been married since his nineteenth birthday and had two small sons. When he sought guidance from a senior church official, his confession was quickly reported to the bishop and he was asked to resign the same day. He made a new life for himself in the Los Angeles area, and after several years, with the encouragement of friends, he became certain that he was called to found a new church where gay people could reach God in an atmosphere of love and acceptance.

That was in 1968. Twelve persons attended the first service, in the minister's home. By the end of the first year five hundred gay men and women, with friends and supporters, met in an old movie theater and together gave ten thousand dollars to purchase a church building. Metropolitan Community Church had become a reality. Since that time, well over 120 study groups, missions, and chartered churches have been formed in every major United States city, as well as in Australia, New Zealand, Canada, Nigeria, and Great Britain, and some three thousand persons attend its general conferences.

Today, in contrast to its modest beginnings, MCC is an ecumenical Christian church open to all people, with a special concern for anyone feeling excluded from or neglected by mainline churches. Its members try to make Christian gospel the focal point of their lives and the binding force in their relationships with one another.

The ceremony of Holy Union, or marriage within the church if not within the law, is a vital means to that end. We have attended several marriages at MCC, and we wish we could share that moving experience with you. At a recent Holy Union in Baltimore, for instance, fifty people crowded the small basement chapel. Two love songs introduced the service, then the couple knelt to receive the minister's prayers and the church's message that love and fellowship are sealed through the love of Jesus Christ. The pair were urged to befriend each other, to be open, to listen to words said and words unspoken; they should respect each other's rights and each allow the other to be an individual, accepting the other for what he is. They are to share life together according to Christ's law of love.

After the vows and exchange of rings came hymns and prayers, followed by a communion service in which the entire congregation participated. The minister gave wine and wafers at the altar, embracing each communicant in turn while speaking a few private words of encouragement or blessing. Couples went up hand in hand and shared the pastor's message as he placed his hands around their shoulders.

Delores Berry, a twenty-six-year-old black woman, has recently been ordained at MCC in Baltimore. She discussed her vocation with us in a taped interview and expressed herself so effectively that we have let her story and her belief speak for MCC in these pages:

When I was twenty-one I was ordained into the Christian Methodist Episcopal Church. I had decided celibacy was the answer. I had figured out that I was gay and I had very negative feelings about gay people. I thought that the Bible held that gay people were sinners, and I knew that they were socially outcast, and I thought they should have been. I hadn't really known any gay people, I just had these ideas that gay women were rough and butchy, unpleasant, and I couldn't see myself being that. Then two gay people came in for counseling; they were forty or fifty years old. I could see the pressure they were under, so I decided to start reading up on the issue. I went to the library and I found out about the gay community, its organizations, newspapers, and books. I had no idea any of this existed. I was so excited, my whole attitude changed. I started smiling at gay people on the street, thinking they were brave—they had nerve and I didn't. . . .

I decided to tell my bishop. The Methodist Church had been ordaining women for years, and the bishop was always saying it was OK for women to be in the ministry. . . . It made me feel bad doing this, coming out, because I knew they would see it as a bad thing for all the women ministers. . . . But then I went to the Metropolitan Community Church. I met a woman minister who said, "I am a lesbian." I couldn't believe she just did that. It made a big impression on me. . . .

I told my bishop and I asked him what the church's position was on the gay issue. He said, "What people do in their own bedroom is their own business," which made me mad: it's not a matter of the bedroom or even the house—it's the world. He said he'd had high hopes for me. He told me not to tell anybody and no one would know. But I told him, "There are too many invisible gay people. I won't go back." He then said I could start a gay church, a branch of the Methodist Church, but later he came back and said that wouldn't be possible. I didn't hear from him for four months. Then he said he couldn't send me to a congregation with older people because they'd be upset, and he couldn't send me to a congregation with young people because I'd influence them, but he could send me to a congregation with no people: starting up my own but without any gay people as officers of the congregation. So I said good-bye.

Now I'd rather do counseling than work from a pulpit. The gay community really needs Christian leadership—an understanding of morals, loving respect for each other, reeducation of biblical views. There are so many gay people who feel negative about themselves, as I did, because they think God is against them. Finding out that's not true is so important. There was this gay organist I met who played the most beautiful organ you can imagine. He was wonderful. I asked him if he'd come play for services at MCC and he said he couldn't play God's music because of what he was. He felt he was going against God by being gay. And there are so many who feel this way. Every day they live and breathe they feel they are going against God. Many have died without knowing that God loves them. We've put ministers, the church, up on a pedestal, but what's needed is answers, Christian guidance, to enable people to get close to God, to take God with them wherever they go. To know that they aren't stained people.

MCC is definitely not only for gay people. Families and friends often find that these warm, supportive congregations provide a congenial atmosphere in which to worship. Our friend June Durham, whose son is gay, serves as a deacon of MCC in Baltimore and is always welcome in the gay men's bars where she does mission work for the church. And sometimes ministers from other denominations feel a special call to work with gay people.

Here are excerpts from a talk given by Kay (see page 51) to her Methodist congregation as she was about to leave them for MCC in Milwaukee, a group that she and her husband had worked hard to establish.

Three years ago I didn't know about the church called Metropolitan Community Church. Three years ago I wasn't aware of the number of gays in our society—10 percent, or twenty million in our nation today. . . . God seems to have called my husband and me into this mission field, to tell these gay men and women that God does truly love them and want them. We have begun to realize the all-encompassing and the all-inclusive quality of God's love and His Kingdom.

It is something like the story of Paul, the Apostle—called by God to be an apostle to the Gentiles, a people he had once persecuted. At first Paul didn't understand the Gentiles but he learned to love them even as his own people in Christ. We, too, have learned to understand and love the gay people; but it took God many, many months to open our minds and hearts; and now today we feel very blessed by God for choosing us to work in this mission field.

We cannot end this chapter without mentioning two nationally active religious groups that are serving Catholic and

Jewish gays in somewhat the same way that MCC serves former Catholics and Protestants. Dignity, the Catholic organization, was founded in San Diego in 1969. By 1972 additional chapters were being set up in other cities; as of this writing more than fifty chapters unite tens of thousands of gay Catholics. A group known as Integrity serves Episcopalian gays.

Father John McNeill, S.J., was active in Dignity's formation. Quoting from the organization's statement of purpose he writes:

> We believe that gays can express their sexuality in a manner that is consonant with Christ's teaching. We believe that all sexuality should be exercised in an ethically responsible and unselfish way.*

> The primary purpose of Dignity is to help the gay Catholic realize that to be Christian he need not deny his homosexuality, but rather he *should* be fully himself in order to be fully Christian. . . . Dignity wants people to accept the fact that because we are human we have the right to use sex in the only way that is natural for us. When that is accepted, we will be seen very easily as morally and physically healthy, patriotic human beings.†

Members of this organization work toward the day when the Church hierarchy will accept as valid the Catholic homosexual's goal: "to affirm his or her sexual orientation in faith, to regard themselves as equal members of the believing community, and to express their sexuality in a manner consonant with Christ's teaching of love."‡

Similar to Dignity in many respects, the movement known as Jewish Gays has spread to most American cities having substantial Jewish populations. Active synagogues with rabbis, cantors, and adult education programs have been maintained in Los Angeles and New York since 1972; the

---

* McNeill, *The Church and the Homosexual,* p. 174.
† Ibid., p. 172.
‡ Ibid., p. 6.

Los Angeles synagogue is now affiliated with the national Reform body, the Union of American Hebrew Congregations.

Metropolitan Community Temple Mishpocheh (meaning "family") of Baltimore and Washington is typical of the smaller, less formally organized groups. Members hold services and Oneg Shabbat every Friday night and on the High Holidays. As one member said of a Yom Kippur service held in another member's home:

It was followed by a joyous break-fast meal and discussion session among almost forty persons unlike any other rap session I had ever been in. People poured their hearts out in grateful communion. It was a reawakening and a reunion. There were women and blacks, teachers, a taxi driver, lawyers, writers, a house painter, retail sales clerks, architects, students, businessmen and civil servants galore, servicemen (army and navy), and more. It was a diversity as wide as the whole city. We had just three things in common:

1. We were Jewish
2. We were gay
3. We felt a need to be among gay Jews on this day

I do not know what others there were thinking. I can tell you what happened to me. Every other time in my life, when we came to the Amidah, the Silent Devotion when we examine our hearts and souls to ask forgiveness for the unrighteous paths we had trod, I wept inside for the gay acts I had done in the year past. I begged for some kind of mystical release from the guilt I felt. In my early years I even begged God to change me. He never did. But my anxieties increased with ever-returning fall.

But this year, I was free. I prayed in grateful thanksgiving in a service that made me feel happy to be alive, thankful to God for the community of men and women who had, at long last, learned to be happy with the way God made us . . . different from other of God's children perhaps, but God's children nevertheless. This is why that service was a new experience, a reawakening for me. As my Baptist roommate says, it was like being reborn. To me, as a Jew, it was *Shalom.*

And in the words of Temple Mishpocheh's statement of purpose:

The group was founded to provide a sense of belonging and understanding that many of us have not been able to find within our own families and synagogues. We have felt alienated and have found that our own particular needs are often ignored. As our rabbis have taught us to do, we as Jews have come together again to express our Jewishness as we never have before.

That final statement might serve to summarize what open acceptance in a religious community means to every gay person who seeks God's love: We want to come together again to express our faith as we never have before.

8

Parents and Children Together

In her novel *Consenting Adult*, Laura Hobson writes of a family that begins in the early 1960s to deal with a son's homosexuality. More than once the mother, Tessa, finds herself rebuffed by both son and husband in her efforts to talk about the matter. Jeff often refuses to discuss any aspects of his life with his mother; and Ken will not give in to his wife's (or his) need to air her feelings. At one point, Tessa reflects that "each one of us . . . is always and forever at the core of our own pain; each one looks outward to others as if they were indeed outside the core." This thought vividly expresses the isolation and unhappiness that a lack of communication creates within families. A somewhat different aspect of it is illustrated as a gay woman writes to her parents: "You must realize, once and for all, *I* will not (and cannot) change—*you* are the ones who must change. I've tried every way I know to help you understand, but you don't seem to hear anything I have said."

Whenever a parent or child will not listen or talk to the

other, the flow of comfort and learning that would help them both is closed off. Coming to an understanding of our gay children is not something we parents can do by ourselves—nor is it something our children can do for us. What a family must do is to work it through together, with as much open communication as possible (listening as well as speaking) and with an honest expression of feelings, questions, and personal experience by both parent and child.

We must point out here that *we* cannot do it for other parents, either. We can relate our personal experiences and convictions and those of others; we can tell you what we have discovered that has been helpful to many parents and to young people. But we cannot change attitudes or unlock firmly closed minds. None of us who work with parents has found a way to reach those who refuse to examine their own attitudes and beliefs.

The people who respond well, who come through it all successfully (and from whom we continue to learn much ourselves), are those who, no matter how distressed initially, are willing to make an effort. Sometimes simply hearing that an open, positive viewpoint is possible can unfold the way to that view.

Finally, we have found that it is not only parents who need help. Gay people themselves want to understand more about how their parents feel and what they can do to help. So, although here as elsewhere we direct ourselves primarily to parents, we are really speaking to both parents and gay children—indeed, to the entire family as other members become involved in the learning process.

At the outset, perhaps our most important word of advice is *relax*. It is not the end of the world; your gay child is not doomed to a life of pain and unhappiness, nor are you. Of course, this aspect of your child's life is something that needs to be talked through, learned about, and dealt with— as openly and comfortably as possible. Nothing is to be gained by hysterical reactions, anger, tension, or a wall of silence—and a great deal can be lost. The fact is that our gay children need our support, not our condemnation or avoidance of the issue.

Since your gay child's primary anxiety is that she or he will be rejected, clearly your first response should be one of reassurance. It's vital to let Terri know that of course you still love her, to assure Ben that you care for him as much as ever—and that you will support them in whatever ways you can. And it's never too late to tell your child that he or she is loved. If you neglected to say this when you were first confronted with the news, you can do so now. And remember—a big hug is powerful two-way medicine!

Actually, there is no valid reason to stop enjoying your gay child as you do all your children; no need to suddenly see your son or daughter as someone "totally different" from the child you knew. We know (and often advise) that young people say to their parents: "I'm the same person I was before I told you this; you just know one more thing about me." Think about it: your child has not "changed" in some terrible way, but has shared with you an essential part of himself or herself. If your love and attention are focused on your child, you can discover and enjoy what being gay means to that child.

For example, Irene and Frank and their four children are entirely at ease with the fact that one daughter is gay. Irene writes:

Kate is a *total* person now. . . . Since she's out of the closet, she's happier, more militant in her crusade for human rights. Both Frank and I are proud of her—and 100 percent support-ive! Her brother and sisters know she's gay and couldn't care less. As for me, I'm watching and enjoying her spirit, her en-thusiasm, even her own wonderment. It's a beautiful kind of metamorphosis, and I wish I could explain to other parents that if their child is homosexual and is delighted and unashamed of the fact, then the parent must also be delighted and unashamed. Or would parents prefer their gay children to be "heterosexual-or-dead"—or miserable—or dishonest?

I think that parents who "understand" share feelings of self-worth and of respect for others—and are not morbidly absorbed with different (which doesn't mean better or worse) kinds of sexuality.

Irene and Frank are not unique; many, many people have told us—and we have found it true ourselves—that when gayness is an open subject, parents and children find greater joy in each other and in themselves. We can all revel in the emerging discoveries of our gay children, if we will.

It is only fair to acknowledge that for a good many of us a relaxed feeling about our gay child is not easy to achieve immediately. Frequently subconscious barriers prevent us from viewing this aspect of our child's life rationally, as we would an unexpected choice of career or heterosexual mate.

For most of our lives, the word *homosexual* has meant for us feelings of terror, revulsion, and fear of the unknown. And when our child suddenly applies that word to herself or himself, we are confronted with other deep-seated feelings, some of them about ourselves.

Very likely we have an overwhelming sense of guilt or failure as parents. The question "Where did we go wrong?" is so common as to have become almost a cliché; even so, it is no less anguishing for each parent who is struck with the question. For many years psychologists (and society in general) have laid the burden of "blame" for all sorts of behavior, individual differences, and developments in children's lives on the shoulders of the parents. But here is what Dr. George Weinberg has written: "Having a homosexual son or daughter in no way implies having failed as a parent. There are between twenty and thirty million parents of homosexuals in this country, many of whom have been unnecessarily demoralized by the propaganda that they are failures."*

* From National Gay Task Force's Gay Parents Support Packet.

Still, even though this environmental theory of personality development is beginning to lose favor, most of us grew up with it so deeply etched on our consciousness that we still assume it is true. In fact, however, gayness is an early, apparently natural, and perhaps inevitable development in some children, and there is no demonstrable proof that we parents are responsible for it.

So for now we encourage you to recall the ways you know yourself to have been—and to be—a good parent, some of which may be evidenced, as one mother says, by "the good things you know about your gay child, the good things he's done, the respect and love for you he's had." We might keep in mind that our children have paid us the triple compliment of love, trust, and faith by sharing this news with us; we can accept this compliment with justified confidence in ourselves as parents.

We can also take comfort from the message that is frequently directed to our own children. As one young man reminds his fellow gays: "Be patient! It will take your parents as long to adjust to your being gay as it took you, so don't expect miracles." We have found that too grim a determination, perhaps laced with resentment at *having* to deal with this, will keep you from achieving an easy, relaxed attitude and enjoyment of your gay child.

A further barrier to a receptive frame of mind arises when we concentrate on what seems lost forever—our hopes and dreams for that child. Most of us have built-in expectations for our children: a successful career, a loving mate, children (*our* grandchildren!), a beautiful home, an active social life, and a respected place in the community. But when our child says, "I'm gay," we may suddenly assume that none of these can ever be realized. The fact is that many of these things are still possible for the gay person who wants them. But we should also understand that *our* dreams are not necessarily our children's (gay or not) dreams; and we might hope our children will achieve what they most want in their lives, rather than fulfilling our expectations.

Remember, too, that you want to do what is best for your child, not what you think she or he needs. A good many parents hasten to rush their child off to a psychiatrist to be "cured," or they consider doing so. When we first meet parents, they often ask us about the possibility of their son or daughter being "changed" and we have several responses to that.

First, we consider the idea of a "cure" to be unrealistic, because homosexuality is not a sickness. It is part of the total personality of an individual and, as far as science is aware today, it develops from the same complex of genetic and environmental factors that determine any other personality trait.

Second, we believe that only when a particular trait causes discomfort or prevents the individual from functioning well in society should one think about trying to alter it. Sexual preference need not fall into this category. Again, it is unaccepting societal attitudes that cause discomfort to gay people, not the sexual orientation itself. These attitudes have been changing for the better in the past several years, so that particularly in urban areas, gay people suffer less discrimination than in the past. As more gays emerge publicly, and as education of the general population continues, discrimination and oppression can be expected pretty much to disappear—and with them the external and internal pressures on the gay person to try to "change."

But the crucial point about cures is that they don't work. Among gay people who have been submitted to shock treatments or to nausea-producing or other aversive techniques intended to condition them against homosexual attraction, the majority never really succeed in becoming entirely heterosexual in their desires, and most acknowledge that they still have strong homosexual feelings. As one gay woman remarked to us: "I've known one or two people who were sent to psychiatrists to be cured of being gay. It never worked. The most that can happen is maybe you can be able to make love with someone of the opposite sex and not get sick, but I don't see the value in that! Shrinks have power in how they manipulate how people see themselves."

We wholeheartedly concur. Any therapist who does not respect the homosexual aspects of an individual's orientation will only aggravate the anxieties and diminish the self-image of a client who is uncomfortable about his or her sexuality. Value judgments, in our opinion, have no place in psychiatry. Therefore, if psychiatric treatment *does* seem indicated (for example, to help your child accept her- or himself as a valid, worthwhile person), it is vital to find a psychiatrist who does not have a bias against homosexual inclinations. But most of the gay people we know like themselves as they are. Therapy is not necessary for everyone.

Related to the idea of "being cured" is the idea of "outgrowing it." Some of us try to believe that our son or daughter has only been experimenting, or has been led astray by someone, and that he or she will become heterosexual "again." In our report from Jim and Mona in Chapter 3, Jim speaks of his initial hope that Rick would "work his way back to heterosexuality." In so doing, he expresses a belief common to many parents—that their gay child started life as heterosexual and can thus go back to it "if they only wanted to," or "if they would just *try*." Yet when any of us focus on this "hope," it keeps us from moving toward real understanding.

While we've provided some rationale for a change in our attitudes, we also know that this cannot be achieved by simple mental decision making, for it comes as a part of the ongoing process of learning to understand your child as a gay person.

So, here are some specific steps to take.

Sharing. Finding someone to talk to who understands your concerns is in itself quite a relief. Just sharing your feelings with another person will release tension and help you feel less isolated. And remember, you are not the only parent in the world with a gay child! Others like you are going through the same things. You may be apprehensive at the idea of talking with strangers about anything so personal, but—believe us!—our own and hundreds of other parents' experience is that it pays off. Parents of Gays groups offer comfortable access to people working in the same direction as yourself. If there is no parents' group in your area, your child's friends can help to find another mother or father who would welcome the chance to learn and share with you. Alternatively, usually there is an informed counselor, therapist, social worker, or minister who can relieve your anxieties and offer helpful suggestions and information. In any case, don't hesitate to call gay organizations or hotlines in your community; the staff people there will be more than willing to talk with you or to refer you to others who can help you.

Reading. If you've gotten this far, we know you don't have to be persuaded to read. But if this is your first book on this subject, we do encourage you to read others. Much excellent material is available—books, pamphlets, audio cassettes, periodicals, newsletters—and more is coming out all the time. Our list at the end of the book includes materials we have found most helpful; your child may have access to others. Many books dealing with gay topics are now available in general-interest bookstores; all of them can be found in or ordered from one or another of the growing number of gay bookstores. If there is one such in your community, we urge you to visit it; not only will you find a wide selection of good reading, but a friendly and helpful atmosphere as well—people who will put you at ease and who will be happy to talk with you.

As you read, we think you'll find the wide variety of life

stories and experiences of lesbians and gay men instructive, interesting, and heartwarming. Some of you will enjoy poetry and fiction by and about gay people. And the discussions of gay issues by psychologists, theologians, historians, gay activists, parents, and others are bound to be reassuring and extremely informative.

You might even want to subscribe to one or·two local or national gay newspapers. These will keep you informed about gay topics of significance to your child and other gay men and women and will provide a variety of current news and information that is interesting and useful to you as a concerned parent.

Meeting. For a good many of us, the various words that mean *homosexual* have called up a variety of vague and unpleasant pictures all our lives. We may be confused and angry as we try to relate the discomforting images to our child. The answer lies in the fact that although our ideas about what gay people are like have very little to do with reality, somehow those "pictures" are likely to linger. The very best way to discard your false impressions about gay people and learn the truth about homosexuality is to get acquainted with gay women and men—meet them, talk with them, get to know them. A lot of us feel apprehensive at first about meeting gay people. But the story changes when we give ourselves a chance! Let two mothers tell us of their experiences. Marguerite speaks of the gay conference she rather hesitantly attended:

I was surprised that the group of young people we were talking with was so nice—open, intelligent faces, asking and answering questions. When I felt my surprise, I realized I had been thinking that Larry (my son) was the only good young man— an exception among all those weird ones. Since then I have met really outstanding gay women and men, and a lot of other pleasant ones, teaching me that the spectrum of human qualities is the same for gay people. I need not fear for my son; he is in good company.

Phyllis Shafer describes how it was for her back in 1957, soon after she learned her son was gay: "One Saturday afternoon Drew brought home seven friends for me to meet, and vice versa. Those poor boys were *scared,* as was obvious from the looks on their faces, and I was too! But I was as pleasant as I could be to them, and, as I had learned a few gay terms, I used them. Well, after that, I was in!"

We recommend especially that you welcome your child's friends into your home. Those "terrible visions" disappear rapidly, you forget that they are supposed to be "different." Of course there are individual differences among gay people—just as there are among nongays. There are many troubled gay people simply because they are members of a stigmatized minority. But we think you will find, as we have, that the majority of the people you meet are attractive and interesting young men and women—open, friendly, and lively—who will be very happy to meet and talk with you. Some will probably become your friends. And when you discover, as many of us parents have, how many gays *cannot* talk freely with their own parents, you will see more clearly what being gay has (so unnecessarily) cost these people. You will feel even more gratitude for your own child's love and trust. More than that, you will want to make sure that your child always feels free to turn to you.

Along with the learning experiences you are having, you will want to find appropriate ways to help your child.

When your children do turn to you, you will want to take care that you respond in ways that make them feel good about themselves. We must be aware that our gay daughters and sons are the victims of oppressive societal attitudes—far more than we! Thus, we must avoid playing on their possible feelings of inadequacy or shame, to help them get along in a world that may at times be difficult.

Positive messages. Sometimes our questions or comments carry hidden messages. For example, how much more positive to ask your child, "How long have you known you were gay?" than to say, "How long have you been 'that way'?" Parents will often say, "When she told me she was *like that...*" or use similar phrases: "that kind of person" or "those people." Try to use the terms they use: lesbian, gay, or homosexual. Our lifetime enculturation has made us uncomfortable with these words; we have been taught to feel that they are shameful, and it is especially difficult to apply them to our children. But we can learn to feel easy about it, and we must. When we use evasive expressions, we convey these very feelings of shame to our children.

Setting standards. There are other ways to help your gay child. Frequently, when a child is still living at home, the parents think they can "solve the problem" by keeping that child away from "bad influences" or from a particular friend. Suddenly there are new rules and regulations: an early or total curfew, restricted telephone use—even listening in on all calls; questions about time spent away from home; and generally an atmosphere of suspicion, distrust, and accusation. (We heard of one mother who began to find fault with everything her gay son did and even seemed to attribute his lack of diligence in carrying out the garbage to his sexuality!) Neither prohibitive measures nor nagging will change your child's sexual orientation! Keeping your child away from his or her friends and setting up new restrictions is surely unnecessary and unfair. All adolescents need to be with their peers, and young gay people in particular need the support and friendship of others like themselves. There is no reason for your gay child to have unlimited freedom, but whatever rules you set for any of your children should suffice for this child as well.

Occasionally parents find that their child has a special friend who is considerably older, and immediately they suspect "the worst"—that the older person has seduced, or "recruited," their child. But one young man told us his first gay experience was with an older man to whom *he* made the overtures, and this is fairly typical. Furthermore, if we can set aside our prejudices and assumptions for a moment, we will see that such a relationship, which in any case may not be sexual, is not necessarily exploitative of your child and can actually be beneficial. Young people often find support and reassurance from an older person. And most of the gay people we know have a sense of responsibility for younger friends; they know what it is to grow up being different, and they want to make it easier for young friends and acquaintances.

We achieve nothing by isolating and distrusting our gay children, except to make them miserable and, often, desperate. And there is so much we can do.

The lover. When your gay child of whatever age tells you there is someone special in her or his life, we hope you will welcome that woman or man into your life. Unfortunately, some parents seem to find this difficult, if not impossible, to do. We hear of those who totally refuse to acknowledge their son's or daughter's lover. One young man told us: "My parents never mention Paul. When I write them about the work we're doing on our house or about Paul's promotion, they never say a word in return. If he answers the phone when they call, they just ask for me in as few words as possible. They have never sent him even a small gift at Christmas time. For them, it's as if he doesn't exist!"

One woman told us about her mother's attitude: "She actually refers to Angie (if at all) as 'that thing'! Can you imagine how that makes me—and Angie—feel? I love Angie deeply—we've been together nearly eight years—and my mother calls her a *thing*."

Other parents may be less extreme, but still they tell their daughter: "We want you to come home for the holidays but don't bring *her*." Gay men tell us of identical experiences with their families.

So many unnecessary barriers are built, so many painful rifts created by these attitudes. Yet *we* know, as do hundreds of other loving parents, that it can be a joyful and rewarding occasion to know the woman or man who is so important to our child. As one mother told a group of parents: "Mindy has the most beautiful woman as a lover . . . and I now have *two* daughters who I love very much." It is true that sometimes our child will fall in love with someone we don't particularly care for, but that certainly happens with our straight children too! We owe it to ourselves and our children to get to know the important people in their lives.

The affectionate touch. As you welcome your child's lover into your home and your life, you may have difficulty accepting any signs of open affection between them. We've heard parents insist they will never be comfortable with the couple's most casual touch—the embrace of greeting, a loving arm across the other's shoulder, even hand-holding—and God forbid that two men should kiss! While we probably feel less aversion to affectionate gestures between women than to those between men, there is the occasional parent who says she cannot bear to see Judy and her lover "touching." Other parents, like Phyllis, have less difficulty with this. She says, "Affection between same-sex couples? I think it's great! I can't see why they should hold in and hide their love for one another any more than straight couples do. . . . I will admit at first it seemed strange to me and I had the feeling that I should look the other way or something. But it never was a problem and it isn't now."

We ourselves have been through this. Betty recalls that

several years ago, Glenn invited me to a large party that he and friends were giving. This was the first time I had seen men (or women) dancing together and exchanging a kiss now and then. At first I felt a little embarrassed, but soon I was having a fantastically good time—chatting and laughing with these young men and women. And long before the evening was over, my feelings of "strangeness" about their hugs and kisses had completely disappeared.

One woman told us that she advised parents who were upset by seeing affectionate gestures to ask their child and his or her lover not to embrace in their presence. This is one option, but we would rather encourage parents to relax and accept this than to place awkward restrictions on our young people.

We think the "problem" with displays of affection is simply this: We are not accustomed to it. Lisa, who described her reaction to her son's homosexuality for us in Chapter 3, makes an interesting point: "I have never had a problem about hugging or kissing in public. My background is Vienna, Austria, and I am used to seeing men embrace each other." But in the United States and Canada, our eyes are not used to it, our minds are not used to it, and our rules seem to forbid it! As a matter of fact, few of us care to witness *any* couple engaged in heavy lovemaking, but we usually don't mind the casual touch or embrace of our straight children or friends. And when we are aware of real affection and love between gay people, our viewpoint changes. We believe that you will find it endearing and heartwarming to see your children express the tenderness and deep feeling that they have for each other.

Appearance. One area where you and your child may have wide differences of opinion is the matter of appearance—clothing, hair, and general grooming. This is often a result of a generation gap and it is not limited to our gay children, but sometimes it aggravates feelings of discomfort parents have about the gay life-style. We find there are no hard and fast rules or advice that can be applied to all families; expectations about dress vary too much, not only between parent and child within a family, but between different families. So we offer a potpourri of comments and opinions which may help you crystallize your own approach to this subject.

The point, basically, in this area and others, is to help

your child feel good about herself or himself. Nagging or criticizing unduly will only work against this goal. And yet, some of us are horrified with the way our gay kids look. Some interesting points are made by an MCC minister.

I'm very familiar with this problem. When they first try to adopt an openly gay life-style they don't know exactly how they want to appear—what kind of image they want to project. Men sometimes want to reject the macho male image and they express their rejection of conventional society by wearing outlandish dress; the women don't want to look feminine because they associate that with trying to appeal to men. Very often both men and women are fighting guilt and self-hatred, and this lack of confidence is reflected in uncared-for-looking clothing and grooming. Confidence and pride in one's appearance go along with the development of an appropriate personal style of dress—but it's the strong self-image that comes first, permitting the development of a distinctive, yet attractive, appearance.

Some parents find that if there is a problem with their gay child's appearance, it comes from another member of the family. Genevieve, divorced fifteen years ago, works in an accounting office; she says, regarding her nineteen-year-old daughter:

I've devoted the last fifteen years of my life to Nell. I never went out or ran around; I've made her my whole life. I believe in her, I love her. We have a wonderful relationship and I know she brags of me to all her friends. I want to help her any way I can! But my problem is with my mother—she won't let Nell in the house! We have a large, close family with frequent gatherings for holiday, Sunday dinner, and so forth, but my mother says for my daughter not to come around until she can look decent. Nell wears sloppy jeans, and lots of times she looks messy—she doesn't wear becoming clothes. My mother makes it so hard for me!

But one thing we can all take heart from, if we're disturbed about how our children dress and look, is that they probably will eventually improve; very likely none of them

will want to go through life looking like a slob. Nancy tells
what developed with Avril:

She used to wear baggy, wrinkled clothes, with her hair pulled
straight back in a rubber band, her shoulders stooped. We could
never expect her to go with us to a nice restaurant—which was
especially embarrassing when our parents or older friends came
to visit! Now, after five years as a gay woman, she wears well-
fitting, stylish shirts that she buys in boutiques (though the
pants might be clean, well-fitted jeans)—no skirts, though. With
her relatively long torso and short legs, she looks much better
in pants. Her hair is short and curly—she's a natural blond and
she's very vain about it, spending up to eighteen dollars every
six weeks to have it cut by a fashionable Georgetown unisex
hair stylist. Her posture is that of a graceful athlete and she
takes beautiful care of her body with diet and exercise. She is
graceful and lithe—perfectly gorgeous. People who know her
have said to me, "What a *waste*"—can you imagine? As though
only men should have the right to enjoy beautiful women!

Irene's daughter Kate took a different route when she
came out. As her mother says, "She used to be 'Kathy,'
with hip-length hair and lots of eye makeup (fooling herself—and us—no doubt?). Now, she's 'boyish,' short-
cropped hair, jeans, etc. As much a uniform and as much
conformity as straights!"

We might note that not *all* gay women wear jeans and
short hair—any more than all nongay women dress like
Farrah Fawcett-Majors. Appearance does tell us something
about how people feel about themselves, but dress style or
hair length (for either women or men) is hardly a realistic
indicator of sexual preference or of personal qualities—
unless "breaking away from the traditional" shows an alert
openness to the validity of individual preference. Betty's
feelings about various aspects of appearance are these:

I have to acknowledge I do like long hair on men. Glenn used
to wear his hair much longer than he does now—fine with me!—
and I've always liked his looks with a beard. As for his style of

dress, it could best be described as casual—for some years, he deliberately avoided any semblance of dressing up. Since neither he nor I have much occasion or wish to go to elegant places, I was never very troubled when he consistently dressed in old flannel shirts or T-shirts and faded jeans. And his employers have never demanded any changes in his appearance. Very recently he has shown more interest in wearing better clothes.

But the point, to me, is that he's a "neat person"—talented, introspective, sensitive to others. These qualities mean far more to me than outer trappings—something I like to think is basically true for most of us.

In the matter of appearance, probably the answer is to try to find some points of agreement with which both you and your children can be comfortable. With a generally positive approach on your part, we hope you will be able to help your child express a good self-image.

Telling others. Sooner or later the question will arise: How do we tell the rest of the family, our friends? Sometimes it's sooner; parents who have just found out will ask us, "But *what* am I going to say to my mother? My sister? How can I tell our other children?" So many of us seem to think that now that *we* know that Bob or Karen is gay, we must immediately let everyone else know. And at the same time, we are terrified that they will find out!

Our advice to parents is: Wait until you feel good about it. If you are hurting and anxious, it's no time to be talking to relatives who are unlikely to take the news well. When you feel that the news from your son or daughter is bad, you are frightened, confused, or ashamed; the news is likely to be received by others in the same way. One thing you don't need at this point is gloomy and pessimistic responses from those around you. But as you feel happier and more accepting, you will be able to present the information so that it calls forth a similar response. Charlotte Spitzer puts it succinctly: "An interesting thing happened. I discovered that when I could tell friends and others about my daughter with my newly gained positive attitude, they also accepted the news in a more positive way."

This view is borne out again and again. One of our friends, who had just learned about her son Philip three days earlier, said in tears, "I don't know how I can tell his older brothers. They'll *kill* him!" But less than three months later, when Ilse had long since given up her own fears and pains, she called to tell us that the previous evening while Philip was out, she had told the two older sons that their brother was gay. They were quite shocked. Yet when Philip came in, his brother went to him, embraced him, and said: "Philip, Mom told us. And we love you as much as ever. You'll have to give us some time to understand this, but we want you to know that our feelings haven't changed for you one bit." Had Ilse talked to her sons earlier when she was still distraught, their response might have been different.

Justine revealed in a lengthy letter that she still has difficulty believing that her daughter Marsha is "really" homosexual. She comments about telling other people and her family's reactions:

I am a blabbermouth, especially when I hurt, and I hurt badly in December and January. Therefore I told several of our friends, but I discriminated enough to know to tell only those I knew would understand not only our position but Marsha's as well—and she has gotten a lot of support from them. My own father we do not intend to tell; however, I think he suspects.

As for our other two daughters, Terry, the middle one, knew the previous summer, as she and Marsha discussed it. She thought, and still does to some degree, that it is a stage resulting from Marsha's rejections both in high school and in college. When the reality came to the fore in December, Terry wrote Marsha a very nasty letter; I begged her not to send it, but she did anyway. This was partly because she saw the way the situation at the time was hurting me, and therefore the others. However, that has resolved itself now, mainly, Terry says, because she thinks Marsha's lover is such a great person.

Our younger daughter, Lynn, visited Marsha at her women's

college in the fall and pretty much saw what the situation was, so it was no surprise to her. However, she did say that it had turned her off to going to that school, that she didn't want to see girls going around embracing, etc. She said that if that was what they wanted to do, it was OK with her—she just didn't want to be around it.

We know that parents cannot always keep the news from other family members until they themselves feel good about it, but it's not hard to see in this case that the other daughters' problems about their sister and about gayness in general may have been reinforced by Justine's own difficulty in accepting the realities. (Several months later Justine wrote again, saying that she and her other daughters had "come to grips" with Marsha's lesbianism and were dealing with it well. Even difficult beginnings are often resolved happily.)

Parents frequently insist that other children in the family, especially the younger ones, must not know. Although there is no way to predict how brothers and sisters will react (any more than gay people can accurately assess their parents' reaction in advance), we have found that often they are more likely to be accepting—even offhand—about the news than parents expect. It may be that the gay person has already talked with them, or that they have guessed and don't care; each generation is more open to new ideas than the previous one. It does happen that older siblings—married and settled into a fairly conservative mode of life—occasionally have more trouble with the news than the younger ones.

But the timing of the telling is really up to the gay daughter or son. If John asks his parents *not* to tell the other children, he probably isn't ready himself to handle their responses, and he shouldn't have to do so until his own feelings of self-worth are stronger. But when Laurie is ready to talk with her siblings (or anyone else in the family), then Mom or Dad's insistence that "nothing be said" is not particularly constructive.

Perhaps the one exception might be very much older

relatives. It's possible that "Grandma and Grandpa would never understand—they're too old and set in their ways." But even here, this is not always the case! Irene writes: "Incidentally, Kate's grandmother (my mom—who's a very foxy lady) doesn't '*know*.' (Gad! you'd think Kate was a murderess!) But only because Kate wants to tell her personally when she visits her soon. Grandma will then probably start a Grandparents of Gays movement!"

We have heard some people say that no one but the gay person has a right to reveal this news to others. This view seems unrealistic to us. Naturally, we should get our child's permission to share this information with brothers and sisters and other relatives and friends, but it doesn't seem practical or necessary to insist that the gay person do all the telling. We see no reason why parents, who need someone to talk to, should not share this news with a trusted and sympathetic relative or friend. Obviously this doesn't mean running around talking about the "shocking news" or "how terrible it is" with people who are sure to regard it that way themselves and to pass it on as the latest gossip! But we hope *you* don't feel that way about your child's gayness, anyway!

The experiences of some other families may help you formulate your own attitudes and decisions.

ANNE: Fortunately I found out that family members can be a great source of strength when they are mature enough to rise above petty bigotries. I have been so fortunate; my sisters (not so my brothers) have been open-minded, and we discuss my son very openly—they love him very much. My nieces are the same, and their fairness and understanding are not extended only to my son, for they are open in their expressions and sympathies toward the gay community as a whole.

I was surprised at first that the fact was not repulsive to them; I thought they would be appalled, but I might just as well have said he was changing jobs for all the difference it made. I think my son is one of the lucky gay people who can be himself with almost every member of his family. This, too, is surprising, because we were brought up to be very prudish, and bigotry was an accepted standard when we were young.

PEG L.: I have never told my parents, who are both eighty-one, about Barry; I haven't told other members of the family in their age bracket either. But members of our own generation, with whom we are fairly close, know. Seven years ago my sister-in-law—who was originally trained as a pediatrician and then went on to raise four kids, then was divorced, and trained as a family therapist—reacted to having Barry tell her about himself with the thought that he should have psychiatric treatment. But she has turned around in the intervening time and her attitudes about homosexuality have changed. I don't know how much Barry had to do with it . . . but she is a terrific person and so dear to all our kids that it was she Barry told first.

We went about telling our friends gradually; there was a strong inclination not to bring it up with people who didn't know Barry, thinking they'd just have some sort of stereotyped picture in their minds—whereas to know this kid is to love him, so I can't imagine anyone thinking less of him because they learned he was homosexual.

Actually we have been here seven years now and a good many of our friends, at church anyhow, do know about Barry, and some have met him. . . . He's been back for two visits, and he went to a parish meeting way back in 1970 to explain discrimination at the church's annual conference. He told them something about homosexuals and the fact that they all know them but didn't know they did. . . . We were still so new to the church then that it was a pretty dramatic moment when he made this little spiel—but we survived it all very well.

PHYLLIS SHAFER: My husband's sister and my brother have no qualms about our son's homosexuality. I told my mother and dad on their fiftieth wedding anniversary, thinking it would be acceptable, as I was always close to my mom and she loved her grandson dearly. However, she reacted the opposite way and didn't want to have anything to do with Drew. I knew she was in "shock," so I told her if she didn't love my son she didn't love me either. Well, that snapped her out of it. She and my dad accepted him wholeheartedly then, and loved his lover also. My mother did ask me not to try to explain it to her, as she was too old to comprehend it all, so I complied with her wishes.

ANN SHEPHERD: We did not want the younger girls to know right away that Susie was gay. When we did tell them, it was fairly traumatic at first, although Jennifer, then seventeen, accepted it pretty matter-of-factly. Gloria, our youngest, was going through a difficult seventh-grade year (when she was twelve and a half) and spent the summer of 1975 in twice-weekly sessions with an excellent child psychiatrist squaring away her own identity as a healthy teenager. This was the best thing we could have done for her, because she is now a very strong young person, sure of her own heterosexuality, with a couple of nice boys she sees in a good boy-girl relationship, *and* with a host of gay men and women friends—the best group of older brothers/sisters any person could desire. In fact, at this time, Gloria is befriending a sixteen-year-old lesbian from another high school, assuring her that she is a real whole person, and feeling her responsibility as a "counselor." Gloria also gave an interview in her school paper last May, detailing what it's like to have a gay sister!

And finally, as you're deciding when and how and whom to tell, we echo Jeff's comment: "Try to introduce a sense of celebration—this kind of sharing is meant to bring people together. Look forward, not backward. And do it with love."

A word to gays. We're pretty sure that the gay women and men who read these pages will draw inferences for themselves from our remarks to parents. As families work their problems out together, each person begins to understand more about the other and the task of working through becomes clearer and easier.

And yet the one question we are constantly asked by lesbians and gay men who have not yet talked with their parents is simply: "How can I tell my parents that I'm gay?" To this question, of course, there is no single—or simple—answer. Although we believe and hope that more and more parents today will accept the news with a relaxed and inquiring attitude, we must acknowledge that some will find this difficult. So although many aspects of the answer to "How do I tell my parents?" are implicit in this chapter and others, we offer a list of suggestions that have proved to be helpful to many other gay people. But remember— there are *no* answers that guarantee instant success with every parent!

1. First, a lot depends on how *you* feel about being gay. If you think it's the greatest, that helps.
2. Choose the time to tell sensibly—when things are going well, or at least when a certain amount of calm prevails.
3. *Don't* blurt it out during an argument; it will become a weapon instead of a sharing.
4. You may want to tell only one parent at first, depending on your relationships with them.
5. Lead into the telling, if you can, with an expression of love and concern for your parents. If you don't usually say these things, think up something nice or thoughtful to say or do.
6. Be prepared for the possibility that the news will upset and hurt your parents, and that one or both of them may lash out at you. Try not to respond defensively and angrily; allow them this initial reaction.
7. Tell them, "You loved me before you knew this. I'm the same person I was then, and I hope you still love me."
8. Keep the lines of communication open, and remember that your parents are having to change their concept of you and your life—and that they probably don't have an accurate picture of what homosexuality is.

9. Read good books on the subject and make them available to your parents.
10. If they cannot deal with this subject rationally, don't force the issue. Don't flaunt yourself or your friends defiantly—but if your parents are willing to meet your friends, make sure they have the chance to do so.

And a final word to parents. Frequently, when we talk to others—parents, gays, nongays—we speak of the need for parents to "come out" themselves. It is just as important for us mothers and fathers to come out of *our* closets, leaving our own isolation and distress, as it is for our children; and as important, to whatever degree we can, for us to speak up for our children and their gay friends and associates. By so doing, we find a new purpose and meaning in our individual lives and we grow in love, self-respect, and human understanding. What's more, we become closer to our own children as familial bonds deepen and strengthen. This is not mere rhetoric; these things have happened to both of us, and they are happening to scores of parents everywhere. Think about it. Can you dare to ask any more for yourself? Or any less?

9

Parents of Gays:
A Group That Works

Paula hesitated before the apartment door. Through the panel she heard a muffled burst of laughter and a man's deep voice speaking. . . . How could they laugh? And how could she come here and meet the unknown hostess politely, go in and *face* all those people? She lifted her hand to knock, then dropped it. I'll just go home, she thought. They'll never know I was here. Then, in the hall behind her, someone passed quietly, and not wanting to be caught standing like an idiot—or a thief—she rapped quickly, decisively. It's done, she thought. I'm here and I've got to go in!

The door opened briskly and Paula faced a tall gray-haired woman in pants and dark pullover. To her surprise, the woman reached out and clasped Paula's arm.

"Hello. You must be Paula Raines. I'm Wilma." She smiled warmly and gestured. "Come on in. We're just about to start."

Through an archway Paula saw a blur of people: several women, a few younger folks, a shirt-sleeved man or two.

They all looked pretty nice at first glance, not strange or threatening. Yet she knew that each of them, like her, had a terrible secret. But as Wilma took her around, they were so friendly and welcoming that she was able to bear being introduced by name. Still, it made her sick inside to realize that just by showing up at this meeting, all these people knew she had a gay child!

The doubts and fears that Paula experienced are common to many parents who've decided that it's time they attended a Parents of Gays meeting. These feelings are, however, dispelled rather rapidly once the initial meeting is under way.

But what *is* Parents of Gays? What does it do for parents of gay daughters and sons? It has been suggested, by those who hear about it, that it must be a support group, or a consciousness-raising group, an educational forum, a political organization, or, by one person, a place where parents can go to "talk about how awful it is to have a gay child." We were asked once, "But what is the POG viewpoint? Do you talk about how to change your child?" Except for the last, Parents of Gays groups are all of the above, in some respects, and perhaps more.

Other questions: How long has POG been in existence, and are there groups in most communities? Are most parents eager to attend such a group once they learn they have a gay child? Are these groups open to "everyone," or are they a kind of elite group for only certain parents? Is there a national organization one can join? Who runs such groups —and what happens in them?

Let's take the history first. As short a time ago as 1972 there was not a single such group. In fact, although increasing interest and attention was directed to the problems young gay women and men were facing—in recognizing their homosexual orientation, in coming out to friends and family, in finding (or founding) a stable gay community in various cities, in employment, relationships, and other facets of (anyone's) life—still, the factors that influenced and disrupted families, particularly in terms of the parents themselves, had been largely unrecognized or ignored.

But suddenly something new happened. In New York City a young gay activist persuaded his parents, Jules and Jeanne Manford, along with Sarah Montgomery (see Chapter 3), to work on getting a group of parents of gay people together. Jeanne, a schoolteacher in Flushing, and her dentist husband, Jules, had gone through some hard times coming to terms with the fact that their son was gay, but they had made it and although they had not yet been particularly activist in this area, they were ready to do something. Sarah, on the other hand, had been working with all her energies for the cause of gay women and men, as she is to this day. These three parents, supported by a number of gay people, set out to gather other parents together, to help alleviate the anguish and pain and fears that so many of them experience.

At the same time efforts were being made in Los Angeles and in San Francisco to start similar organizations. And in May 1974—in a move that ultimately led to the writing of this book—Betty Fairchild scheduled the first meeting of POG of Washington, D.C. This group drew parents primarily from surrounding Maryland and Virginia suburbs; it is still in existence, now meeting in separate locations in Maryland, D.C., and Virginia.

Shortly thereafter, parents in other cities began similar projects. Jean Smith, who had been one of the original members in Washington, D.C., moved with her family to Pensacola, Florida, and began efforts to meet other parents there. Because of her husband's position in the military, her efforts were forced to be anonymous (Jean Smith is the name she uses as a contact). Against great odds, Jean has worked valiantly to spread the word that it's OK to be gay; she gathers literature and writes letters and disseminates them widely through a monumental mailing list, and she is continually pressing city, state, and federal officials and university, church, and civic groups for acceptance of gays. (Jean, like other parents working for gay issues, receives no funding for her work and, like them, considers her extensive out-of-pocket expenses a part of her contribution to the cause.) While no active parents' group has evolved in military-oriented Pensacola, Jean's work continues and she is now being invited to speak on gay issues in other cities.

In Minneapolis in September 1975, Betty was invited to speak at a conference of the Minnesota Committee on Gay Rights. One of the few parents attending this meeting was a mother who was so inspired by hearing about a group for parents that she determined to start one in her city. Supported by gay organizations and leaders, POG-Minneapolis is now one of the most active and well-attended in the country. A recent, and as far as we know unique, project of the group was a one-day workshop for parents from outlying communities who live too far away to attend monthly meetings.

Parents of Gays and Lesbians in New York and Parents and Friends of Gays in Los Angeles are now large and active, with a variety of activities, including helping individuals in other communities start their own groups. Long Beach, California, has a good group going, with a large attendance by both parents and gay people. Dave Cassidy, a young gay activist in Montreal, has just begun a bilingual POG group there and he hopes to find a parent to take it over soon. And we have just heard of the formation of a POG in Edmonton, Alberta. POG is now international.

In addition to such groups, there are parents in a number of cities and towns (and in some cases young gay women and men) who serve the extremely important function of being POG "contacts," making themselves available to other parents or young gays, to talk with and counsel them on an individual basis.

How often we have heard a young person ask, "Is there a POG group in my hometown? My mom really needs someone to talk to." For all too long, the answer has had to be, "Sorry. I'm afraid not." But as time passes and word spreads, we discover more and more sympathetic parents who say, "Yes, you may use my name as a contact."

For some, like Mona and Jim in St. Louis and Kay and Lloyd in Wisconsin (see Chapter 3), it is a new direction. "We still have some problems ourselves," says Jim. "But we felt that we were ready to move out and do something to help." It is not easy for parents, especially at first, to put themselves on the line this way—to have their names published (if only in a limited way) across the country—but these parents are aware of how important it is for gay people and their parents to learn that there is *somebody* they can talk to in their community.

As noted earlier, Kay and Lloyd have not found other parents to meet with, or even to talk to; instead, they are devoting their time and loving concern to working with young people and with other organizations and people in their community and nearby Milwaukee. Thus, they remain important contacts for POG in their state.

What a delight it was to discover Phyllis Shafer, who has been doing this very kind of work for more than twenty years—long before any sort of general public attention was given to homosexuals. She says,

I feel that God intended this to be my life's work, what is left of it (I am seventy years old), helping gays and parents of gays. I am a "contact" for POG here in Kansas City, and hope soon to get into counseling on a regular basis. It has been my dream to help others get over their heartache, as I know exactly what they are going through—I've been there.

And in Springfield, Oregon, as we found out in early 1977, there is a woman who has also learned to know and care for gay people, and to talk with them and some of their parents in a helpful and understanding way. A pastor and his wife in a small midwestern town, whose daughter is a licensed MCC minister in Colorado, have long been willing to speak with other parents, if they will only come forward. And Lisa, in Ohio, has spent years counseling young people as they face the problems of being homosexual in our restrictive society.

We won't try to mention each and every one involved (and we could not possibly know of all those individuals who are working on their own to help—but we would like to hear from them!). To our knowledge, at this writing there are fifty-four groups or contacts for Parents of Gays in twenty-seven states, and at least five in Canada and England. It is surely heartening to realize that there are so many parents (as well as gay women and men), known to us or unsung, who are devoted to helping other parents, and to changing conditions, not only for their own gay children, but for all gay people.

But, how do POG groups help? What are they actually doing?

Although there is not yet a "national organization," and each group is formed independently, there is an increasingly strong network of Parents of Gays, as they communicate with each other, work to encourage and establish new groups wherever sympathetic and willing parents become known, and share newsletters and information that will be helpful to each other. The common goals, although not formally articulated for all groups, are to help parents develop a new perspective toward homosexuality in general and toward their gay child in particular.

Some groups meet in churches or other community centers; others, especially while they remain small, meet in members' homes. Wherever they gather, the atmosphere is friendly and informal, conducive to sharing feelings and experiences and to getting to know each other.

The striking experience for the new parents at a POG meeting is the chance to speak, often for the first time, of having a gay daughter or son. Most parents have, naturally, felt an overwhelming isolation; they may have been living with constant fear and shame and guilt, without anyone to talk to or to receive sympathetic understanding and comfort from. So when a mother like Paula comes to her first meeting, she is likely to be baffled that the other parents can laugh, and she may say somberly, "I just found out about Peter last week, and I don't feel much like laughing." The others in the group instantly surround her with understanding and comfort. "We know—we all cried, too. But the wonderful thing is, we know that in a few weeks you'll feel better."

"I have a gay son, too," one says. "I thought I'd never be able to accept it—but I have. And you can, too."

And the talk goes on along these lines, moving to various individual stories, detailing the successes or achievements our gay children have experienced and what problems they still face. Paula finds herself immensely relieved of the terrible inner pressure that has been torturing her. Not that she can immediately "understand" her son's sexual preference—but she knows for the first time that she is not alone, that other women and men are dealing with the same feelings and doubts as she.

Just as many young gay people initially feel as if they are the "only ones," parents, too, perhaps even more so, feel isolated and unable to express (and consequently even to identify) their feelings. While there may be some talk initially, as one questioner suggested, of "how awful it is" to have a gay child, the emphasis of all Parents of Gays groups is on encouraging parents to discard that feeling and to gain understanding and pride, to *re*gain closeness to that child.

We find that most parents feel that there are three important steps to take at POG meetings. Sharing feelings and experiences with others is the first step toward change. We begin to see some of the negative feelings we have had drop away as it no longer—at least with these people—is a secret.

The next step: By meeting and getting to know a variety of gay people at these meetings, parents begin to shed their stereotypical images of the sorts of people their own children must be associating with, as well as, of course, what kind of person they think their own daughter or son is doomed, in their minds, to be.

By talking with these young people, asking questions that we can't ask of our own gay child, by hearing articulate and well-informed answers, by hearing about these people's experiences in life, parents begin to learn what it means to be gay today. We learn where these young people work, how their lives are going, what their problems have been, what they want to do with their lives, and along with it all, we see that they are not so different from all our young people—a real revelation! Not all the answers are good news; there is still a lot of pain and difficulty. But we begin to know that not all the bad things we've heard about happen to *all* gay people, and we are reassured because these young people seem well adjusted, with the usual complexity of interests and goals that we are all familiar with.

A third step is learning how many organizations are now present on both the local and national level. At first, most parents hardly know that a gay community exists, much less how many gay people are providing such services as rap or coming-out groups, coffeehouses, gay rights activities, gay youth groups, free VD clinics, counseling/therapy, legal and medical referrals, Gay Alcoholics Anonymous, gay parents' groups, child custody assistance, churches, synagogues, and other religious institutions. It is certainly reassuring to realize that all gay people are not cruising the streets and bars, and that our own children may find companionship, support, and help in good, stable surroundings.

———

How do the meetings themselves run? There's humor, talk, exaggeration, friendship. Parents sit and talk and find the relief provided by the meetings can be a wonderful feeling. But some groups go farther than inviting only parents: they invite special guests whose expertise on the subject may be of particular interest to parents and their children, broadening our scope of understanding of a subject so few of us know much about. And many groups make available a growing library of good, positive, interesting books; new ones are coming out all the time and these, too, add to our comprehension of the variety and scope of gay life. Parents with religious objections can be directed to some of the excellent and persuasive new treatments of this topic, one too complex and specialized for most of us to discuss in detail during the course of a meeting.

All these activities do not take place at every meeting, of course. And there are some variations from group to group. Some groups rarely have special speakers, but rely on their own sharing and learning for growth. Others, such as the New York and Los Angeles groups, where the attendance is large and consists primarily of parents who have been attending for some time, usually have two events each time: the first, for "parents only," in which they can talk of personal problems; and the second, a program meeting with a presentation of some kind and discussion.

Whatever happens, whatever positive viewpoints are shared, we cannot overemphasize the need for repetition, for saying (and hearing) the same things again and again, for meeting with a variety of gay people over a period of time, in order for change to take place. We point out to young people that they must give their parents time to assimilate this new information; the same is true for parents in POG: most of us need a lot of time (and repeated experiences) to absorb and accept this total reversal of all we've been taught is right and normal, and to refocus our expectations for our gay child.

Some parents cannot rid themselves of particular prejudices. For several months Florence L. continued to ask: "But why? *Why* did this happen to my son? He has always been such a dear and loving person." Even though acknowledging when challenged that he is still a dear and loving person, until Florence began to see and hear other parents accepting that their child could be dear, and loving, and gay, she could not stop asking why.

In Florida a father asked again and again: "Do you think there's a chance my daughter will change?" When he could not get the answer he wanted ("Yes"), he could not hear the positive things that were being said to him. So in the discussions at POG, simple answers to questions do not always solve the problem. The combination of ongoing experiences, the ability to allow one's assumptions to be challenged, and to accept concepts that seem totally contrary to those assumptions, all work toward understanding, if the parent is open to it.

Furthermore, some parents will come to POG to share their acceptance and understanding. One mother told of her son's coming out this way:

Well, actually, I told him that he was gay. Tim had been very unhappy, had been engaged to a nice young woman once, and had broken it off . . . and then he was living at home for a while, and I could see that he was upset most of the time. And although he was still dating a little, he'd say, when the phone rang, "If that's Cathy, tell her I'm not here." I knew, for longer than he suspected, what his difficulty was. So one evening I called up an older man we both knew—he was gay, and like a member of our family—and I asked him to come over to talk with Tim and me. We all sat around the dining table, and eventually I said, "Honey, why don't you give in to your true feelings? I think your real interest lies in men. . . ." Not in just those words, but that was the idea. Tim just sat there, with a kind of rueful smile on his face. Rich, our friend, chimed in, too, with some good words of friendly reassurance. It was so great to see Tim beginning to acknowledge what he had been hiding from himself for so long. And now—he has the finest young man as lover. I love them both dearly.

Rita and Ken, both in their sixties, are always full of enthusiasm and interest at meetings, perhaps bringing in relevant news clippings or an article, or telling of a letter to the editor on gay issues that one of them has written. On their first visit to POG, they shared with the group the fact that they have only two children, both sons, and both gay. They told how their sons' revelations (coming at different times) were difficult to hear, but that through a real determination to learn what this way of life meant to their sons, and with a lot of love and caring in their relationship with the two young men, they had indeed come to understand and appreciate their sons' lives.

Other parents, hearing these stories, cannot help but be influenced by parents who now accept their gay children so well.

Another phenomenon occasionally occurs. One evening, Lee, who was there for the first time, was speaking in some anguish of having known for six months that her son was gay, having dealt badly with it that whole time.

"I don't even know why I'm here," she said. "Jack asked me to come and I did, but I know I'm never going to understand his being . . . like that."

There were murmurs of sympathy, when suddenly Barbara, who had been experiencing similar difficulties herself for some time, spoke up.

"Listen," she said with surprising enthusiasm, "I know just how you feel. But you just keep coming to these meetings and I *know* you're going to look at it differently. Why, all of us here have gone through the same thing— and look at us! We're beginning to feel really good about our gay kids!" Then she looked around and said in amazement, "Did you hear what I just said?"

"Terrific, Barb," someone said.

"Why," Barbara added, "I didn't even know I felt that way!"

What do parents themselves have to say about the value of Parents of Gays to themselves and to others?

Lillian K. writes:

My relationship with my daughter is excellent. She says I'm a "neat lady." I think she gives me more credit than I'm due. After all, I don't have to deal with the situation publicly, with her living three thousand miles away. I will say, though, I've come a long way—thanks to her and to the POG group.

Rosa B:

When I first started coming to these meetings, I needed them desperately. And now [more than a year later] I still look forward to them. In a way, I sort of need my "fix"—I always get a real high from hearing all the reassuring things that go on and from being with other parents who are working on this situation. And also, I'm beginning to realize that I can help them, too, that because I've been through it all, I have something to offer. And that is part of the high!

June (during a talk she gave at a gay rally):

What about the parents who may think, but are not sure, that their daughter or son is homosexual? Talking with us in this group might help make it easier to communicate honestly with their child.

Betty, who has worked with POG in both Washington, D.C., and Denver, has said many times that her experiences with the two groups have been very rewarding:

Even though we always wish we could reach more parents (sometimes the small attendance is discouraging), still, the knowledge that all of us who are working in POG may have pointed the way, or opened up new vistas, for even *one* parent, one family, makes it all worthwhile.

How do gay children themselves feel about Parents of Gays? We have rarely talked with gays who were not enthusiastic and supportive of the concept. "I wish I could get my parents to come," they say. Or, "If only there were a group in my hometown!" Or, "I'm going to see if I can't get my mother to your next meeting!"

When Betty left Washington for Denver, she was more than gratified to receive the following letter from the then-president of Gay Activists Alliance of Washington, D.C.:

I didn't want to let you get away from Washington without sending you my warmest best wishes—both from myself and from GAA.

All of us are sorry to see you go. We can't begin to tell you how much you and your work has meant to us. Your contribution to better relations between gay people and the nongays cannot be exaggerated.

Of course I am particularly grateful to you for helping me and my parents during my coming-out period. I think life for all of us has been a lot better thanks to you.

Furthermore, the young people who attend POG meetings with their parents, as they occasionally do, or those who come to share with other parents, if not their own, find much encouragement in knowing that there *are* parents who will try, and they gain new insights into what parents are thinking and feeling—something they may not have seen too clearly before. The sharing between parents and gay people is beneficial to both.

Now that we have seen POG as a group that can and does work, we want to talk about how interested parents can go about forming such an organization. Ideally, every community of whatever size should have this resource available, for as we've noted before, gay people (and their parents) are a part of our society everywhere. We believe that there are parents in many cities and towns, as yet unknown to us, who with a little help from their friends (us) would be willing to get a Parents of Gays group going, if they only knew how. Most of us have learned by doing, but we don't propose that the wheel be reinvented again and again. So although we make no guarantees of success (there is no surefire formula), we have gathered together some suggestions for the parent or couple who may never have worked in gay-related areas. First, we might say, be prepared for your life to change—for the better, and to your enrichment. Promoting a parents' group takes hard work and dedication, but the rewards are many.

Now, what to do:

1. Find out if there are gay organizations in your community. Check the phone book for "gay" listings, and call any or all for further information, telling them who you are and why you want to know. Check also for an MCC (Metropolitan Community Church), Dignity, and/or Integrity— all gay religious groups which, like other gay groups, should be interested and supportive. Find out if there are local gay publications.

2. Start publicizing your interest in starting POG with all gay groups and persons you locate. Ask them for their assistance and ideas. If possible, meet with such groups or individuals to make yourself known and to get to know them. Encourage them to refer "potential" parents to your group.

3. As soon as possible publicize a phone number where someone (preferably you as a sympathetic parent) will accept calls, answer questions, talk with troubled or inquiring parents and/or young gays. You might want to arrange to use the number of an organization that will refer calls to you, to avoid any unwelcome calls. (Betty notes that she has always used her own phone number and has not been troubled by more than a few bothersome calls. Most other parents who list their home number find this to be true, too.) But it is important, in fact vital, to provide a warm and personal contact for callers.

4. Other ways to publicize POG: print up an inexpensive flyer announcing formation of POG; send it to all gay

groups, to churches, mental health centers, hospitals, social service agencies, and to similar groups, individuals, and centers, as well as to daily and gay papers; put it up on bulletin boards. If there is no local gay paper, you might want to put a notice in one of the nationally read gay papers. Send public service announcements to all broadcast stations (some will use them; some won't). Radio, TV, and newspapers seem to be increasingly open to presenting short segments on this topic, so you may be able to obtain some talk show or press feature publicity.

5. As soon as you hear from as few as two or three interested parents, set a meeting date and continue to hold regular meetings. (Otherwise you may lose those initial inquirers.) Don't worry about "programs" at this point; just get together informally. Clarify, in your own mind and with the others, realistic goals for the group.

6. Meanwhile, read (see the Bibliography for recommendations). Inform yourself and broaden your own viewpoint. You may want to subscribe to one or more of the national gay newspapers or periodicals to learn of current news and developments on gay issues and to learn more about gay life today.

7. Start to collect a library of "good reading for parents." Most people will be willing to borrow (and return!) books that they might not purchase themselves. (Be sure to have them sign them out, so you'll know where the books are.)

8. Invite one or two lesbians or gay men to your meetings very soon. Encourage gay sons and daughters (and other children) of group members to attend.

9. Meetings for relatively small numbers of people (which is what you'll have for a while) held in someone's home provide an informal, intimate, and friendly environment, and also offer privacy. However, if a group becomes too large for this (oh, happy day!), you may want to ask a church, library, or other community center to make a meeting place available.

10. You'll find yourself spending your own money, so once you start meeting regularly, you should explain this and not be timid about asking for voluntary contributions to defray mailing, advertising, publicity, and library costs.

11. *Don't be discouraged if initial and continuing response is slow!* It may take two or three months to hear from a *single* parent. But be prepared to start hearing from gay people with family problems or questions.

12. Incidentally, don't worry if you're not expert in counseling. Few parent-leaders start off as experts, and we learn as we go. And no matter how much experience we have, we surely can't solve all problems. But we—and you—can point the way to clarifying the issues and set the caller on a path to some resolution. So speak from your heart, and know that just "being there" for others is what most troubled people need and appreciate.

13. And finally, all of us in this ever-growing parent-oriented movement offer our heartfelt good wishes and encouragement to you who are about to embark on the greatest and most rewarding adventure of your lives!

Bibliography

NOTE: This list does not include *all* of the good gay literature available, but it does include most of the material that we have found helpful to us and to other parents.

BOOKS

Abbott, Sidney, and Love, Barbara. *Sappho Was a Right-on Woman.* New York: Stein & Day, 1972.
   Readable, pertinent discussion of gay women; how it really is; revealing account of lesbians and the women's movement of a few years ago; much on "becoming an independent and whole person," applicable to nongay women.

Bailey, Derrick Sherwood. *Homosexuality and the Western Christian Tradition.* Hamden, Conn.: Archon Books, 1975.
   Scholarly account of research into the historical foundations of Judeo-Christian attitudes toward homosexual behavior.

Bell, Alan R., and Weinberg, Martin. *Homosexualities: A Study of Diversity among Men and Women.* New York: Simon & Schuster, 1978.
   A look at differences between men and women, with reference to how they describe themselves on the Kinsey scale as to their feelings and experiences. Summary measures are based on emotional and physical responses as well as behavior. Data are compared with those of other researchers.

Brown, Howard. *Familiar Faces, Hidden Lives.* New York: Harcourt Brace Jovanovich, 1976.
   An exceptionally moving account of a variety of lives, including his own, by one of the first doctors to acknowledge his homosexuality publicly.

Churchill, Wainwright. *Homosexual Behavior among Males: A Cross-Cultural Approach.* Englewood Cliffs, N.J.: Prentice-Hall, 1967.

Examines homosexual behavior in various societies and discusses the implications of sexual restrictions. Technical, but important for the serious reader.

Clark, Don. *Loving Someone Gay.* Millbrae, Calif.: Celestial Arts, 1977.

A knowledgeable and matter-of-fact guidebook for anyone who cares about "someone gay"—whether another gay person, parents, spouses, friends, or children of gay people. A must for parents.

Clarke, Lige, and Nichols, Jack. *I Have More Fun with You Than Anybody.* New York: St. Martin's Press, 1972.

A delightful yet serious account of two young men's relationship and experiences. Includes good times together, problems met and solved, family reactions, activity in early gay liberation, and much personal philosophy. Good initial reading.

Gearhart, Sally, and Johnson, William R. (eds.). *Loving Women-Loving Men: Gay Liberation and the Church.* San Francisco: Glide Publications, 1974.

Offers a helpful perspective to those who are troubled by biblical references about homosexual behavior. Excellent overview of the conflict between organized religion and gays, with various views on the subject.

Hobson, Laura Z. *Consenting Adult.* New York: Doubleday & Company, 1975.

A troubled young man reveals to his mother that he is homosexual. An exceptionally fine novel of resulting family conflicts and their eventual resolution. A must for parents—and others.

Hutchinson, Bill. *Now What?* Center for Dialog of Dade County, Inc., 2175 NW 26th St., Miami, FL 33142 ($3.50). Available by mail only.

Written especially for parents, this is easy to read, readily understood, and comprehensive, answering questions that we all have. Good first reading.

Katz, Jonathan (ed.). *Gay American History.* New York: Thomas Y. Crowell Co., 1977.

Comprehensive, informative, widely available, these volumes are exactly what the title implies, marking the place that gay people have in our past—unknown to most of us, but important.

Kopay, David, and Young, Perry Deane. *The David Kopay Story.* New York: Arbor House, 1977.

The personal life story of the first professional athlete, a well-known football player, to come out as gay. Readable and moving.

Kosnik, Anthony; Carroll, William; Cunningham, Agnes; Modras, Ronald; and Schulte, James. *Human Sexuality: New Directions in American Catholic Thought.* A study commissioned by The Catholic Theological Society of America. New York: The Paulist Press, 1977.

The section on homosexuality presents the progressive views of some liberal Catholic theologians. Authoritative and thorough.

McNeill, John J., S.J. *The Church and the Homosexual.* Mission, Kans.: Sheed Andrews and McMeel, 1976.

This Jesuit priest/scholar's intensive study and analysis of the subject, in terms of theology, biblical study, ethics, and morality. A powerful presentation, and a must for those who seek understanding.

Martin, Del, and Lyon, Phyllis. *Lesbian/Woman.* New York: Bantam Books, 1972.

A forthright, warm, understanding presentation by two women who have been on the scene for a number of years and who helped establish a national lesbian organization. Full of verve and humor. Highly recommended.

Nicolson, Nigel. *Portrait of a Marriage.* New York: Bantam Books, 1973.

An intimate and sensitive portrayal of the author's parents —his mother, Vita Sackville-West, in particular.

Perry, Troy, and Lucas, Charles L. *The Lord Is My Shepherd and He Knows I'm Gay.* New York: Bantam Books, 1973.

The founder of the international Universal Fellowship of Metropolitan Community Churches relates simply and readably how his homosexuality and his personal Christian commitment led him through troubled times to acceptance and far-reaching action.

Silverstein, Charles. *A Family Matter: A Parent's Guide to Homosexuality*. New York: McGraw-Hill, 1977.
An introductory book for parents to discuss with their gay son or daughter. Good references.

Simpson, Ruth. *From the Closets to the Courts*. New York: A Richard Seaver Book/The Viking Press, 1976.
Incorporates the author's personal experiences as an active feminist and analyzes the impact on lesbians of various societal institutions.

Tobin, Kay, and Wicker, Randy. *The Gay Crusaders*. New York: Paperback Library, 1972. Out of print in this edition, but reprinted by the Arno Press (New York) in 1975 series.
Biographical sketches of key people in the early gay movement, describing their family ties and relationships; excels in illustrating the diverse backgrounds from which gay people emerge. Hard to find, but worth the trouble.

Tripp, C. A. *The Homosexual Matrix*. New York: McGraw-Hill, 1975.
(Some disagreement here, so we give two assessments.)
a. Filled with unsupported generalities. Has an antifemale flavor when not completely ignoring women.
b. Offers a unique perspective on homosexuality (and hetero-). Although perhaps not a "first book" to read, it is excellent for those who wish to delve into a variety of viewpoints.

Vida, Ginny (ed.). *Our Right to Love*. A Lesbian Resource Book. Englewood Cliffs, N.J.: Prentice-Hall, 1978.
Much in this wide-ranging book for all women (and men, too): gay, lesbian, parents of lesbians—whoever. Excellent articles, viewpoints, and personal stories that broaden our understanding of ourselves and others.

Warren, Patricia Nell. *The Front Runner*. New York: William Morrow & Company, 1974. A sensitive novel frankly and understandingly portraying the love between a mature man and his young protégé. Dignified, touching, and persuasive.

PAMPHLETS

"Twenty Questions about Homosexuality." National Gay Task Force, 80 Fifth Avenue, New York, NY 10011. (Write for information, 68¢ prepaid.) Good answers to all the questions everyone asks.

"Parents of Gays." (Available from Lambda Rising, 2012 S St. NW, Washington, DC 20009; $1 + 35¢ p/h.) Describes early activities and achievements of one parents' group. Discusses common feelings and various responses of parents. A positive approach to homosexuality and helpful hints to both parent and child.

AUDIO CASSETTE

"Counseling Parents of Gays." Fr. Paul Shanley, 1975. (Available from Ampro, Inc., 101 Tremont, Boston, MA 02108, $7.95.)

This Catholic priest addresses parents of gay men, in particular, but his message is helpful to all. Discussion of homosexuality, myths and stereotypes, homophobic attitudes. Shows how and why a parent can and must be supportive of the gay child. A reassuring perspective.

ADDITIONAL RESOURCE

A Gay Bibliography, prepared by Task Force on Gay Liberation, American Library Association. (Available from Barbara Gittings, Box 2383, Philadelphia, PA 19103; 75¢.) This periodically updated publication lists nonfiction books, bibliographies, directories, articles, pamphlets, periodicals, audiovisuals, and special collections.